The Eco-Friendly Guide to Waste Management

Simple Steps for a Cleaner, Healthier World

Osmond Mendez

The Eco-Friendly Guide to Waste Management

TABLE OF CONTENTS

Chapter 1: Understanding Waste Management

The Basics of Waste Management

Waste management, an essential aspect of modern living, involves the systematic administration of waste from its inception to its final disposal. This process includes the collection, transportation, treatment, and disposal of waste, alongside the monitoring and regulation of waste management practices. Understanding the fundamentals of waste management is crucial for creating sustainable systems that mitigate environmental impact and promote human health.

Historically, waste management practices have evolved significantly. In ancient civilizations, waste was often discarded in open pits, a method that posed severe health risks and environmental challenges. Over time, as populations grew and urban areas expanded, the need for more organized waste disposal systems became evident. The Industrial Revolution marked a turning point in waste management, as mass production and consumption led to increased waste generation. This era saw the introduction of landfills and incineration as primary methods of waste disposal. However, these methods often resulted in pollution and environmental degradation, highlighting the need for improved waste management strategies.

One of the most significant advancements in waste management has been the recognition of its environmental impact. Waste, when improperly managed, can lead to soil, water, and air pollution, adversely affecting ecosystems and human health. Landfills, for instance, can produce leachate, a liquid that seeps into the ground, contaminating soil and groundwater. They also emit methane, a potent greenhouse gas contributing to climate change. Incineration, while reducing waste volume, can release harmful pollutants into the air, posing risks to both the environment and public health. These challenges underscore the importance of implementing sustainable waste management practices that minimize environmental harm.

Globally, waste management practices vary widely, influenced by factors such as economic development, cultural attitudes, and governmental policies. In many developed countries, waste management systems are well-established, incorporating advanced technologies and comprehensive regulatory frameworks. Recycling and composting are common practices, supported by public awareness campaigns and government incentives. In contrast, developing countries often face challenges in implementing effective waste management systems due to limited resources and infrastructure. In these regions, informal waste collection and disposal are prevalent, posing significant health and environmental risks. Despite these challenges, innovative solutions and international collaborations are emerging to improve waste management practices worldwide.

Legislation plays a vital role in shaping waste management policies and practices. Governments at various levels enact laws and regulations to ensure the safe and efficient handling of waste. These legal frameworks set standards for waste collection, transportation, treatment, and disposal, and establish penalties for non-compliance. Legislation also promotes waste reduction and resource recovery through measures such as recycling mandates and landfill diversion targets. Additionally, international agreements, such as the Basel Convention, aim to regulate the transboundary movement of hazardous waste, ensuring its environmentally sound management. Through these legal mechanisms, governments can drive progress toward sustainable waste management and protect public health and the environment.

Waste management is a complex, multi-faceted process that requires a comprehensive understanding of its various components. It involves not only the physical handling of waste but also the social, economic, and environmental factors that influence waste generation and disposal. By addressing these factors and implementing effective waste management strategies, societies can reduce their environmental footprint and promote a healthier, more sustainable future.

Efforts to improve waste management often focus on the waste hierarchy, a framework that prioritizes waste prevention and minimization over disposal. The hierarchy emphasizes the importance of reducing waste at its source, reusing materials whenever possible, and recycling or composting organic waste. Disposal, such as landfill or incineration, is considered a last resort. By adhering to this hierarchy, individuals and organizations can make more sustainable choices in their waste management practices.

Education and public awareness are critical components of effective waste management. By raising awareness about the environmental impact of waste and the benefits of sustainable practices, individuals and communities can be empowered to make informed decisions about their waste generation and disposal. Public education campaigns, school programs, and community initiatives can all play a role in fostering a culture of environmental stewardship and responsibility.

Technological advancements are also playing a significant role in transforming waste management practices. Innovations in waste treatment technologies, such as anaerobic digestion and waste-to-energy systems, offer new opportunities for resource recovery and energy generation. Additionally, digital tools and data analytics are being used to optimize waste collection and transportation, improving efficiency and reducing costs. These technological developments are paving the way for more sustainable and innovative waste management solutions.

Collaboration and partnerships are essential for advancing waste management practices. Governments, businesses, and communities must work together to develop and implement effective waste management strategies. Public-private partnerships can facilitate the development of infrastructure and services, while community engagement can foster local support and participation in waste reduction initiatives. By working together, stakeholders can overcome barriers and drive progress toward more sustainable waste management systems.

Ultimately, waste management is a shared responsibility that requires collective action and commitment. By understanding the basics of waste management and embracing sustainable practices, individuals and communities can contribute to a cleaner, healthier, and more sustainable world. The journey toward effective waste management is ongoing, demanding continuous innovation, collaboration, and education. As societies evolve and adapt to new challenges, waste management practices must also evolve, ensuring a sustainable future for generations to come.

Historical Perspectives on Waste Disposal

The history of waste disposal is a tale of humanity's evolving relationship with the environment. From rudimentary beginnings to the sophisticated systems of today, waste disposal practices have undergone significant transformations, reflecting changes in societal values, technological advancements, and environmental awareness. To truly appreciate the journey of waste management, one must delve into the historical context that has shaped our current practices.

In ancient times, waste disposal was an uncomplicated affair. Early humans, living in small, nomadic communities, produced minimal waste, which was easily assimilated by the natural environment. Organic waste decomposed naturally, while inorganic materials were rare and often repurposed. As human settlements grew and became sedentary, the need for more organized waste disposal systems emerged. Archaeological evidence from ancient civilizations, such as Mesopotamia and Egypt, indicates the existence of basic waste management practices, with waste being collected and deposited in designated areas outside city boundaries.

The ancient Greeks and Romans further advanced waste disposal techniques. In Athens, a law was enacted around 500 BCE requiring waste to be disposed of at least a mile from the city. The Romans, known for their engineering prowess, constructed elaborate sewer systems, such as the Cloaca Maxima, to manage wastewater and reduce the risk of disease. Despite these advancements, waste disposal remained a rudimentary process, with many urban areas plagued by unsanitary conditions and frequent outbreaks of disease.

As the Middle Ages dawned, waste management practices regressed significantly. The collapse of the Roman Empire led to a decline in urban infrastructure, and waste was often discarded indiscriminately onto streets and waterways. This period, characterized by poor sanitation and overcrowded living conditions, saw the rise of numerous public health crises, including the infamous Black Death. In response, some medieval cities began to implement rudimentary waste removal systems, employing "rakers" to collect and dispose of waste outside city limits.

The Industrial Revolution marked a pivotal moment in the history of waste disposal. The rapid urbanization and industrialization of the 18th and 19th centuries led to an unprecedented increase in waste production. Factories spewed pollutants into the air and water, while burgeoning urban populations generated vast quantities of domestic waste. The challenges of managing this waste spurred innovations in waste disposal technologies and practices. In England, Edwin Chadwick's report on sanitary conditions in the 1840s highlighted the dire need for improved waste management, leading to the establishment of the first public waste collection services.

The emergence of landfills as a primary method of waste disposal can be traced back to this era. Originally conceived as simple dumping grounds, landfills evolved into more sophisticated systems designed to contain and manage waste. The introduction of incineration as a waste treatment method also gained popularity during this period, as cities sought to reduce waste volume and mitigate the spread of disease. However, these practices often led to environmental pollution, prompting calls for more sustainable solutions.

The 20th century ushered in a new era of waste management, characterized by growing environmental awareness and the development of regulatory frameworks. In the wake of environmental disasters and public health concerns, governments worldwide began to enact legislation to address waste disposal issues. The United States, for instance, passed the Resource Conservation and Recovery Act in 1976, establishing guidelines for waste management and promoting recycling and resource recovery. Similar initiatives were adopted in Europe and other regions, paving the way for more sustainable waste management practices.

The latter half of the 20th century also witnessed the rise of the environmental movement, which played a crucial role in shaping modern waste disposal practices. Public awareness campaigns, such as Earth Day, highlighted the environmental impact of waste and encouraged individuals and communities to adopt more sustainable habits. The concept of the "three R's" – reduce, reuse, recycle – gained traction, emphasizing the importance of waste minimization and resource conservation.

Technological advancements have further transformed waste disposal practices in recent decades. Innovations in recycling technologies, waste-to-energy systems, and landfill management have improved the efficiency and sustainability of waste disposal. The development of biodegradable materials and eco-friendly packaging has also contributed to reducing the environmental impact of waste. Additionally, digital technologies and data analytics are being used to optimize waste collection and processing, enhancing the overall effectiveness of waste management systems.

As we reflect on the historical perspectives of waste disposal, it becomes evident that the journey has been one of continuous adaptation and innovation. While significant progress has been made, challenges remain, particularly in addressing the growing waste generated by modern consumer societies. The lessons of the past serve as a reminder of the importance of sustainable waste management practices and the need for ongoing collaboration and innovation.

The evolution of waste disposal is a testament to humanity's resilience and ingenuity. By understanding the historical context of waste management, we can better appreciate the complexities of modern waste disposal systems and the importance of adopting sustainable practices. As we continue to develop new solutions and technologies, the goal remains the same: to protect our environment and ensure a healthier, more sustainable future for all.

The Environmental Impact of Waste

The environmental impact of waste extends beyond mere aesthetics, infiltrating ecosystems, altering natural processes, and posing significant threats to both wildlife and human health. From the moment waste is discarded, it begins a journey that can lead to far-reaching consequences, affecting soil, air, and water quality in complex and interdependent ways. Understanding these impacts is crucial for developing sustainable waste management practices and mitigating harm to the planet.

A primary concern with waste is its potential to pollute soil and water. When waste is not properly managed, hazardous substances can leach into the ground, contaminating soil and groundwater. This leachate, a toxic liquid formed when rainwater filters through waste, carries with it a cocktail of pollutants, including heavy metals, organic compounds, and pathogens. Once these contaminants enter the soil, they can disrupt microbial communities, reduce soil fertility, and pose risks to agricultural productivity. Moreover, contaminated groundwater can seep into rivers and lakes, impairing aquatic ecosystems and threatening the quality of drinking water sources.

The air is not immune to the adverse effects of waste. Landfills, a common method of waste disposal, are significant sources of methane, a potent greenhouse gas that contributes to climate change. Methane is produced during the anaerobic decomposition of organic waste, and its impact on global warming is estimated to be over 25 times greater than that of carbon dioxide over a century. In addition to methane, landfills can release volatile organic compounds and other pollutants into the atmosphere, degrading air quality and posing health risks to nearby communities. Incineration, another method of waste disposal, also contributes to air pollution by emitting particulate matter, heavy metals, and dioxins, which can have serious health implications.

The environmental impact of waste is further compounded by its effect on biodiversity. Improper waste disposal can lead to habitat destruction, threatening the survival of countless plant and animal species. For instance, marine ecosystems are particularly vulnerable to plastic waste, which can entangle marine life, be ingested by animals, and disrupt entire food chains. The Great Pacific Garbage Patch, a massive accumulation of plastic debris in the Pacific Ocean, serves as a stark reminder of the devastating impact of waste on marine environments. On land, waste can attract pests and invasive species, which can outcompete native flora and fauna, leading to a loss of biodiversity.

The issue of electronic waste, or e-waste, has emerged as a significant environmental challenge in recent years. E-waste, which includes discarded electronic devices such as smartphones, computers, and televisions, contains hazardous materials like lead, mercury, and cadmium. When improperly disposed of, these substances can leach into the environment, contaminating soil and water and posing serious health risks to humans and wildlife. Additionally, the informal recycling of e-waste in developing countries often involves unsafe practices, such as burning or acid leaching, which release toxic chemicals into the air and soil.

In light of these environmental impacts, the importance of sustainable waste management cannot be overstated. Reducing waste generation, promoting recycling and composting, and improving waste treatment technologies are all essential strategies for minimizing the ecological footprint of waste. By adopting the waste hierarchy – which prioritizes waste prevention, reduction, and resource recovery over disposal – individuals, businesses, and governments can work together to mitigate the environmental impact of waste.

Public awareness and education are crucial components of effective waste management. By understanding the environmental consequences of waste, individuals can make informed choices that contribute to a more sustainable future. Simple actions, such as reducing single-use plastics, composting organic waste, and supporting local recycling programs, can have a significant impact on reducing waste and protecting the environment. Moreover, engaging communities in waste reduction initiatives fosters a sense of shared responsibility and encourages collective action.

Technological innovations also play a vital role in addressing the environmental impact of waste. Advances in recycling technologies, such as chemical recycling and automated sorting systems, have the potential to increase the efficiency and effectiveness of resource recovery. Waste-to-energy technologies, which convert waste into electricity or heat, offer a sustainable alternative to traditional disposal methods by reducing waste volume and generating renewable energy. Furthermore, the development of biodegradable materials and eco-friendly packaging can help reduce the environmental impact of waste, particularly in the context of plastic pollution.

Governments and policymakers have a critical role to play in promoting sustainable waste management practices. By enacting legislation and regulations that encourage waste reduction, recycling, and resource recovery, governments can drive progress toward a more sustainable future. Incentives for businesses to adopt environmentally friendly practices, such as extended producer responsibility programs and green certifications, can further support these efforts. International cooperation and collaboration are also essential for addressing transboundary waste issues and sharing best practices and technologies.

The environmental impact of waste is a complex and multifaceted challenge that requires a comprehensive and collaborative approach. By understanding the interconnectedness of waste and the environment, we can develop strategies that not only mitigate harm but also promote a more sustainable and resilient future. Through education, innovation, and policy, we can work together to reduce the environmental footprint of waste and protect the planet for generations to come.

Global Waste Management Practices

Waste management is an essential component of urban living, with practices varying significantly across the globe. The diversity in approaches is influenced by a myriad of factors, including economic development, cultural norms, geographic conditions, and governmental policies. Examining global waste management practices offers valuable insights into the challenges and innovations that shape how societies handle waste.

In many developed countries, waste management systems are characterized by advanced technologies and comprehensive regulatory frameworks. These nations often prioritize waste reduction, recycling, and resource recovery, driven by public awareness and government incentives. For example, Germany is renowned for its robust recycling system, with a recycling rate that surpasses 65%. This success can be attributed to the country's stringent waste management laws, which mandate the separation of waste at the source and impose penalties for non-compliance. Additionally, Germany's deposit return scheme for beverage containers has significantly reduced litter and increased recycling rates.

Japan offers another example of effective waste management, rooted in a culture of meticulous sorting and recycling. The country has implemented an extensive waste separation system, requiring residents to sort waste into numerous categories, including burnable, non-burnable, and recyclable items. This rigorous approach is supported by public education campaigns and community involvement, fostering a sense of responsibility and environmental stewardship. Furthermore, Japan's waste-to-energy facilities play a crucial role in reducing landfill use and generating renewable energy from waste incineration.

In contrast, many developing countries face significant waste management challenges due to limited resources, infrastructure, and regulatory frameworks. Informal waste collection and disposal are common, with waste often being dumped in open spaces or waterways, posing severe health and environmental risks. However, innovative solutions are emerging in these regions, driven by both necessity and creativity. In India, for instance, the concept of "zero waste" communities is gaining traction. These communities aim to minimize waste generation and maximize resource recovery through composting, recycling, and upcycling initiatives. By engaging local residents and businesses, zero waste communities are fostering a culture of sustainability and resilience.

In Africa, the informal waste sector plays a vital role in waste management, with millions of people making a living by collecting, sorting, and recycling waste. While this sector provides essential services, it often operates under hazardous conditions, lacking access to protective equipment and formal recognition. To address these challenges, some African countries are implementing initiatives to integrate informal waste workers into formal waste management systems, providing training, resources, and support. These efforts aim to improve working conditions, enhance waste management efficiency, and promote social inclusion.

In Latin America, waste management practices vary widely, reflecting the region's diverse economic and cultural landscape. Brazil, for example, has made significant strides in waste management, particularly in the area of recycling. The country boasts a thriving recycling industry, supported by an extensive network of cooperatives that collect and process recyclable materials. These cooperatives, often comprised of marginalized communities, play a crucial role in reducing waste and generating income. By leveraging public-private partnerships and community engagement, Brazil is working to improve waste management infrastructure and promote sustainable practices.

The concept of circular economy is gaining momentum worldwide, influencing waste management practices and policies. This approach emphasizes the importance of designing products and systems that minimize waste and maximize resource recovery. By closing the loop on resource use, the circular economy seeks to create a sustainable and regenerative system that benefits both the environment and the economy. Countries such as the Netherlands and Sweden are at the forefront of this movement, implementing policies and initiatives that promote circular economy principles and drive innovation in waste management.

International collaboration is essential for addressing the global waste management challenge. Cross-border initiatives, such as the Basel Convention, aim to regulate the transboundary movement of hazardous waste and promote environmentally sound management practices. By fostering cooperation and knowledge-sharing, these initiatives help countries develop and implement effective waste management strategies that protect human health and the environment.

The role of technology in shaping global waste management practices cannot be overstated. Innovations in waste treatment technologies, such as anaerobic digestion and advanced recycling methods, offer new opportunities for resource recovery and pollution reduction. Digital tools and data analytics are also transforming waste management systems, enabling more efficient waste collection, processing, and monitoring. By harnessing the power of technology, countries can enhance their waste management capabilities and achieve more sustainable outcomes.

Public awareness and education are critical components of effective waste management. By raising awareness about the environmental and social impacts of waste, individuals and communities can be empowered to make informed choices and adopt sustainable practices. Public education campaigns, school programs, and community initiatives all play a role in fostering a culture of environmental responsibility and stewardship.

The diversity of global waste management practices highlights the complexity of the challenge and the need for tailored solutions. While there is no one-size-fits-all approach, the sharing of best practices and lessons learned can help countries develop and implement effective waste management strategies. By embracing innovation, collaboration, and education, we can work together to address the global waste management challenge and create a more sustainable future for all.

The Role of Legislation in Waste Management

Legislation plays a pivotal role in shaping effective waste management systems, driving practices that safeguard public health and protect the environment. Through a framework of laws and regulations, governments establish parameters that guide waste generation, handling, treatment, and disposal. These legal measures ensure compliance, promote sustainable practices, and encourage innovation in waste management.

One of the fundamental aspects of waste management legislation is the establishment of standards for waste treatment and disposal. These standards delineate acceptable methods for handling various types of waste, from municipal solid waste to hazardous materials. By setting clear guidelines, legislation helps prevent the improper disposal of waste that can lead to environmental contamination and public health hazards. For instance, regulations often require landfills to implement liners and leachate collection systems to prevent pollutants from seeping into the groundwater. Similarly, incineration facilities are mandated to control emissions, ensuring that harmful substances are not released into the atmosphere.

Another critical component of waste management legislation is the promotion of waste reduction and resource recovery. Many countries have adopted policies that prioritize the minimization of waste generation and the recycling of materials. Extended Producer Responsibility (EPR) is one such policy, which holds manufacturers accountable for the entire lifecycle of their products, including post-consumer waste management. By incentivizing producers to design products with recycling and disposal in mind, EPR encourages the development of sustainable products and reduces the burden on waste management systems.

Recycling mandates are another legislative tool that promotes resource recovery. These mandates require municipalities and businesses to recycle specific materials, such as paper, glass, metals, and plastics. By diverting recyclable materials from landfills, these policies help conserve natural resources, reduce energy consumption, and lower greenhouse gas emissions. Some regions have implemented landfill bans on certain materials, further encouraging recycling and composting efforts.

Legislation also plays a crucial role in regulating the management of hazardous waste. Hazardous waste, which includes materials that are toxic, corrosive, flammable, or reactive, poses significant risks to human health and the environment. To mitigate these risks, governments have enacted stringent regulations governing the storage, transportation, treatment, and disposal of hazardous waste. These regulations often require facilities to obtain permits, maintain detailed records, and adhere to strict safety protocols. By ensuring the safe and responsible handling of hazardous waste, legislation helps protect communities and ecosystems from potential harm.

In addition to national legislation, international agreements play an important role in waste management. The Basel Convention, for example, regulates the transboundary movement of hazardous waste and promotes environmentally sound management practices. By establishing a global framework for waste management, the convention encourages countries to collaborate and share best practices, ultimately strengthening global efforts to address waste-related challenges.

Public participation is a vital aspect of waste management legislation. Many laws include provisions for community involvement in the decision-making process, ensuring that the voices of local residents are heard and considered. Public consultations, hearings, and comment periods provide opportunities for individuals and organizations to express their concerns and contribute to the development of waste management policies. By fostering transparency and accountability, public participation helps build trust and support for waste management initiatives.

Enforcement is a key component of effective waste management legislation. Without proper enforcement mechanisms, laws and regulations are unlikely to achieve their intended outcomes. Governments employ various strategies to ensure compliance, including inspections, monitoring, and penalties for violations. Fines, sanctions, and other punitive measures serve as deterrents, encouraging individuals and organizations to adhere to waste management requirements. Additionally, some jurisdictions offer incentives, such as grants or tax breaks, to reward compliance and encourage voluntary participation in waste reduction programs.

Education and awareness campaigns are often integrated into waste management legislation to promote sustainable practices and encourage public engagement. By raising awareness about the environmental impact of waste and the benefits of waste reduction, recycling, and composting, these campaigns empower individuals and communities to make informed choices. Educational initiatives may include school programs, public workshops, and informational materials that provide practical guidance on waste management practices.

Legislation also plays a role in fostering innovation and research in waste management. By providing funding and support for research and development, governments can drive the advancement of new technologies and solutions. Research grants, innovation hubs, and partnerships with academic institutions and industry stakeholders help facilitate the development of cutting-edge waste management techniques. These efforts contribute to the evolution of more efficient and sustainable systems, ultimately benefiting both the environment and the economy.

The role of legislation in waste management is multifaceted and dynamic, adapting to the changing needs and priorities of society. As new challenges and opportunities arise, governments must continually assess and update their legal frameworks to ensure they remain effective and relevant. By fostering collaboration, innovation, and public engagement, legislation can drive progress toward a more sustainable and resilient waste management system.

Ultimately, the success of waste management legislation depends on the collective efforts of governments, businesses, communities, and individuals. By working together and adhering to established guidelines, stakeholders can contribute to a cleaner, healthier, and more sustainable future. Legislation serves as a guiding force, shaping the practices and behaviors that will protect our planet for generations to come.

Chapter 2: The Principles of Eco-Friendly Waste Management

The 5 R's: Refuse, Reduce, Reuse, Recycle, Rot

In a world increasingly aware of environmental challenges, the 5 R's—Refuse, Reduce, Reuse, Recycle, and Rot—serve as a guiding framework for sustainable living. Each element of this hierarchy represents a step towards minimizing waste and conserving resources, ultimately fostering a more sustainable relationship with our planet. By understanding and implementing the 5 R's, individuals and communities can make meaningful contributions to waste reduction and environmental protection.

Refuse is the first and perhaps most crucial step in the journey toward sustainability. By consciously choosing to refuse unnecessary items, we can significantly reduce the amount of waste we generate. This begins with saying no to single-use plastics, excessive packaging, and disposable products that contribute to environmental degradation. For instance, carrying reusable bags, bottles, and utensils can dramatically decrease the demand for disposable alternatives, preventing them from ending up in landfills or oceans. Refusing is about making intentional choices that prioritize the environment over convenience, challenging the consumerist mindset that drives overconsumption.

Reduce focuses on minimizing the overall consumption of goods and resources. By being mindful of our purchasing habits, we can cut down on waste production and lessen our environmental impact. This involves buying only what we need, opting for products with minimal packaging, and choosing high-quality items that are built to last. Reducing also extends to energy and water conservation, where simple actions like turning off lights when not in use or fixing leaky faucets can have a significant cumulative effect. By embracing a minimalist lifestyle and prioritizing quality over quantity, we can conserve natural resources and reduce our ecological footprint.

Reuse emphasizes the importance of finding new purposes for items that might otherwise be discarded. This approach not only extends the life of products but also reduces the demand for new materials, conserving resources and energy. Reusing can be as simple as repurposing glass jars for storage, donating clothing to charity, or repairing broken items instead of replacing them. Creative reuse, or upcycling, adds an element of innovation, transforming waste materials into new and valuable products. By fostering a mindset of creativity and resourcefulness, we can reduce waste and promote a culture of sustainability.

Recycle, perhaps the most well-known of the 5 R's, involves processing materials to create new products. Recycling conserves resources, reduces landfill waste, and decreases pollution associated with the extraction and processing of raw materials. While recycling systems vary by location, common materials include paper, glass, metals, and certain plastics. To maximize the effectiveness of recycling efforts, it's important to understand local recycling guidelines and properly sort materials. Additionally, supporting products made from recycled materials helps close the loop, creating a demand for recycled goods and encouraging further recycling initiatives. While recycling is an essential component of waste management, it should be viewed as a complement to, rather than a substitute for, the other R's.

Rot, the final R, refers to the natural process of composting organic waste. By allowing food scraps, yard waste, and other biodegradable materials to decompose, we can create nutrient-rich compost that enriches soil and supports plant growth. Composting reduces the volume of waste sent to landfills, where organic materials can produce harmful methane emissions. Whether through backyard composting, community composting programs, or municipal organic waste collection, composting is an accessible and effective way to manage organic waste. By returning nutrients to the earth, we can support sustainable agriculture and reduce reliance on chemical fertilizers.

Integrating the 5 R's into daily life requires a conscious shift in mindset and behavior. It involves questioning the necessity of each purchase, seeking alternatives to disposable products, and adopting habits that prioritize sustainability. While individual actions may seem small, their collective impact can drive significant change, influencing markets, policies, and cultural norms.

Education and awareness play a critical role in promoting the 5 R's. By understanding the environmental implications of our consumption patterns, we can make informed choices that align with sustainable values. Educational initiatives, community workshops, and public awareness campaigns can all contribute to a deeper understanding of the 5 R's and their benefits. By sharing knowledge and experiences, individuals and communities can inspire one another to adopt sustainable practices and create a ripple effect of positive change.

Businesses and organizations also have a crucial role to play in supporting the 5 R's. By adopting sustainable practices, such as reducing packaging, using recycled materials, and implementing take-back programs, businesses can lead by example and drive demand for sustainable products. Corporate social responsibility initiatives can further encourage businesses to integrate the 5 R's into their operations, promoting environmental stewardship and consumer trust.

Government policies and regulations can support the implementation of the 5 R's by providing incentives for waste reduction and resource conservation. Legislation that encourages recycling, supports composting programs, and reduces single-use plastics can create an enabling environment for sustainable practices. Additionally, government investment in infrastructure and education can facilitate the widespread adoption of the 5 R's, ensuring that communities have the tools and resources needed to succeed.

The journey toward a sustainable future is an ongoing process, requiring dedication, collaboration, and innovation. By embracing the 5 R's, we can take meaningful steps toward reducing waste, conserving resources, and protecting the environment for future generations. Together, we can create a world where sustainability is not just an aspiration, but a way of life, ensuring a healthier planet for all.

Life Cycle Assessment and Waste

Life Cycle Assessment (LCA) is a powerful tool used to evaluate the environmental impact of a product or process throughout its entire lifespan—from raw material extraction to disposal. By providing a comprehensive view of a product's environmental footprint, LCA enables individuals, businesses, and policymakers to make informed decisions that minimize waste and promote sustainability. Understanding the role of LCA in waste management is crucial for identifying opportunities to reduce waste and improve resource efficiency.

The journey of any product begins with the extraction of raw materials. This initial phase can have significant environmental impacts, including habitat destruction, resource depletion, and pollution. LCA examines these impacts by assessing the energy, water, and raw materials required for extraction and processing. By identifying resource-intensive stages, companies can explore alternative materials or practices that reduce environmental harm. For instance, choosing recycled materials over virgin resources can significantly decrease energy consumption and waste generation.

Once raw materials are extracted and processed, they enter the manufacturing phase. This stage involves transforming materials into final products, often requiring substantial energy and generating waste byproducts. LCA evaluates the environmental costs associated with manufacturing, such as emissions, waste production, and water use. By analyzing these factors, manufacturers can identify inefficiencies and implement cleaner production techniques. Innovations such as lean manufacturing, which focuses on waste reduction and process optimization, can help minimize waste and enhance sustainability.

Transportation is another critical component of a product's life cycle that contributes to its environmental impact. The movement of raw materials, components, and finished products requires fuel, leading to greenhouse gas emissions and air pollution. LCA assesses the transportation footprint, taking into account the distance traveled, mode of transport, and fuel efficiency. To reduce transportation-related waste and emissions, companies can explore strategies such as optimizing supply chain logistics, sourcing materials locally, and investing in low-emission vehicles.

The use phase of a product's life cycle offers opportunities to influence waste generation and resource consumption. During this stage, the environmental impact is determined by factors such as energy efficiency, durability, and maintenance requirements. LCA analyzes these aspects to identify ways to extend product lifespan and reduce energy use. Designing products for longevity, repairability, and energy efficiency can significantly decrease waste and resource consumption. For example, energy-efficient appliances reduce electricity demand and greenhouse gas emissions, while durable and repairable products lessen the need for frequent replacements.

Ultimately, every product reaches the end of its useful life, entering the disposal phase. This stage is critical for waste management, as it determines how materials are recovered, reused, or discarded. LCA evaluates disposal options, such as recycling, composting, incineration, and landfilling, to identify the most environmentally friendly solutions. By prioritizing waste diversion and resource recovery, businesses and consumers can minimize landfill waste and reduce the environmental footprint of disposal.

The insights gained from LCA can drive innovation and inform decision-making at multiple levels. For businesses, LCA provides a framework for designing sustainable products and processes, enhancing brand reputation, and meeting regulatory requirements. By understanding the environmental impact of their operations, companies can set targets for waste reduction and resource efficiency, demonstrating a commitment to sustainability.

For policymakers, LCA offers valuable data to inform regulations and policies that promote sustainable waste management. By understanding the life cycle impacts of products and processes, governments can develop incentives and regulations that encourage waste reduction, recycling, and resource conservation. Policies that support eco-design, producer responsibility, and green procurement can drive market transformation and foster a culture of sustainability.

Consumers also play a vital role in the life cycle of products. By making informed purchasing decisions, individuals can influence market demand and drive change. Choosing products with lower environmental footprints, supporting companies that prioritize sustainability, and advocating for responsible waste management practices all contribute to reducing waste and promoting a circular economy.

Implementing LCA in waste management requires collaboration and a willingness to embrace change. Businesses, governments, and consumers must work together to share data, knowledge, and best practices. By fostering a culture of transparency and accountability, stakeholders can collectively address the challenges of waste management and create a more sustainable future.

Education and awareness are essential for the widespread adoption of LCA practices. By raising awareness about the benefits of LCA and providing training and resources, organizations can empower individuals and businesses to incorporate LCA into their decision-making processes. Educational initiatives can include workshops, seminars, and online courses that provide practical guidance on conducting LCA and interpreting results.

Technological advancements also play a crucial role in the application of LCA. The development of software tools and databases has made it easier for businesses to conduct LCA and access relevant data. These tools streamline the assessment process, enabling organizations to identify opportunities for waste reduction and resource efficiency more effectively. As technology continues to evolve, LCA will become even more accessible and integrated into business practices.

Ultimately, LCA is a transformative tool that can drive meaningful change in waste management and sustainability. By providing a comprehensive understanding of the environmental impacts of products and processes, LCA empowers stakeholders to make informed decisions that reduce waste and conserve resources. Through collaboration, innovation, and education, we can harness the power of LCA to create a more sustainable and resilient future for all.

Sustainable Consumption and Production

Sustainable consumption and production (SCP) represent a fundamental shift in how societies utilize resources and manage waste. This transformation is becoming increasingly vital as populations grow and environmental challenges intensify. SCP aims to do more and better with less, promoting resource efficiency and sustainable lifestyles that ensure future generations have access to the resources they need. By understanding and embracing SCP principles, individuals, businesses, and governments can collaboratively create systems that are not only economically viable but also environmentally and socially responsible.

At the heart of sustainable consumption lies the consumer's power to influence market trends and push for change. Every purchase decision carries implications for the environment and society. By choosing products that are sustainably made, consumers can significantly reduce their ecological footprint. This involves selecting items with minimal packaging, opting for products made from recycled or renewable materials, and supporting companies with transparent and ethical supply chains. Brands that adhere to fair trade principles or have clear sustainability certifications often reflect a commitment to SCP, making them preferable choices for conscientious consumers.

Educating consumers about the environmental impact of their choices is crucial for promoting SCP. Awareness campaigns, labeling initiatives, and community workshops can equip individuals with the knowledge needed to make informed decisions. By understanding the lifecycle of products—from production to disposal—consumers can appreciate the broader impact of their consumption habits. This awareness fosters a culture of responsibility and encourages the adoption of sustainable practices such as reducing waste, conserving energy, and supporting local economies.

Businesses play a critical role in advancing sustainable production. A shift towards SCP requires rethinking traditional business models to prioritize sustainability alongside profit. This begins with designing products that are durable, repairable, and recyclable, reducing the need for frequent replacements and minimizing waste. Companies can also innovate by adopting circular economy principles, where products are designed for continuous reuse and recycling, effectively closing the loop on resource use.

Resource efficiency is another cornerstone of sustainable production. By optimizing the use of energy, water, and raw materials, businesses can reduce their environmental impact while enhancing competitiveness. Techniques such as lean manufacturing, which focuses on minimizing waste and maximizing value, can lead to significant resource savings. Additionally, adopting renewable energy sources and improving production processes can further reduce a company's carbon footprint and contribute to SCP goals.

Supply chain management is another area where businesses can make substantial contributions to SCP. By ensuring that suppliers adhere to sustainable practices, companies can influence the entire production network. This involves assessing suppliers for environmental performance, labor conditions, and ethical standards. Building strong relationships with suppliers and investing in capacity-building initiatives can help create a sustainable and resilient supply chain that aligns with SCP principles.

Governments play an essential role in fostering an environment where SCP can thrive. Policy measures such as regulations, incentives, and education programs can drive the adoption of sustainable practices across sectors. Governments can implement regulations that limit resource extraction, encourage waste reduction, and promote the use of sustainable materials. Additionally, fiscal incentives such as tax breaks or grants for green technologies can stimulate innovation and investment in sustainable production.

Public procurement is a powerful tool for promoting SCP. By prioritizing sustainable and ethically sourced products in government purchasing decisions, public authorities can create demand for sustainable goods and services. This not only supports green industries but also sets an example for private sector actors and consumers, demonstrating the feasibility and benefits of SCP.

International collaboration is key to advancing SCP on a global scale. Initiatives such as the United Nations' 10-Year Framework of Programmes on Sustainable Consumption and Production provide a platform for countries to share best practices, knowledge, and resources. By working together, nations can address common challenges, align policies, and drive progress towards global sustainability goals.

Education and capacity building are fundamental to promoting SCP across all levels of society. Integrating sustainability into school curricula, vocational training, and professional development programs can cultivate a new generation of environmentally conscious individuals and professionals. By equipping people with the skills and knowledge needed to implement SCP, society can foster innovation and creativity in addressing environmental challenges.

Technology and innovation are crucial enablers of SCP. Advances in digital tools, data analytics, and sustainable technologies offer new opportunities for improving resource efficiency and reducing waste. For example, smart systems can optimize energy use in buildings, while advanced manufacturing techniques can create products with minimal environmental impact. By embracing technological innovation, businesses and governments can accelerate the transition to SCP and unlock new economic opportunities.

Community engagement and grassroots initiatives play a vital role in advancing SCP. Local communities, non-governmental organizations, and grassroots movements can drive change by advocating for sustainable policies, promoting awareness, and implementing local sustainability projects. Community-led initiatives such as urban gardens, repair cafes, and zero-waste events demonstrate the power of collective action and inspire others to adopt sustainable practices.

The transition to sustainable consumption and production is a complex but necessary journey that requires the concerted efforts of individuals, businesses, governments, and communities. By embracing SCP principles, we can create systems that prioritize environmental stewardship, economic resilience, and social equity. Through collaboration, innovation, and education, we can build a sustainable future that meets the needs of present and future generations, ensuring a healthy and thriving planet for all.

The Importance of Waste Segregation

Waste segregation is a cornerstone of effective waste management, ensuring that different types of waste are properly handled and processed. By separating waste at its source, we can enhance recycling efforts, reduce landfill burden, and minimize environmental harm. Segregation is not merely a technical process; it involves behavioral changes, infrastructure development, and education, making it a comprehensive approach to sustainable waste management.

The process of waste segregation involves categorizing waste into distinct streams, typically including recyclables, organic waste, hazardous materials, and general waste. Each of these categories requires unique handling and disposal methods to maximize resource recovery and minimize environmental impact. By understanding the importance of waste segregation, individuals and communities can contribute to a cleaner and more sustainable environment.

Recyclables, such as paper, glass, metals, and certain plastics, form one of the primary categories in waste segregation. By separating these materials from general waste, we can ensure they are diverted to recycling facilities rather than ending up in landfills. Recycling conserves natural resources, reduces energy consumption, and lowers greenhouse gas emissions associated with the production of new materials. Effective segregation enhances the quality of recyclable materials, ensuring they can be efficiently processed and transformed into new products.

Organic waste, including food scraps and yard trimmings, is another critical category in waste segregation. When organic materials are sent to landfills, they decompose anaerobically, producing methane—a potent greenhouse gas. By segregating organic waste and directing it to composting facilities, we can significantly reduce methane emissions and create nutrient-rich compost. This compost can enrich soil, support sustainable agriculture, and reduce the need for chemical fertilizers, contributing to a more sustainable food system.

Hazardous waste, such as batteries, paints, and chemicals, poses significant risks to human health and the environment if not properly managed. Segregating hazardous waste ensures it is handled by specialized facilities equipped to safely process and dispose of these materials. Proper segregation prevents the contamination of soil and water resources, safeguarding ecosystems and communities from potential harm.

The benefits of waste segregation extend beyond environmental protection, offering economic and social advantages as well. By improving the efficiency of recycling and waste processing, segregation can reduce waste management costs for municipalities and businesses. Moreover, it can create jobs in the recycling and waste management sectors, contributing to local economies and fostering sustainable development.

Implementing waste segregation requires a multi-faceted approach, involving infrastructure development, policy support, and public education. Governments and municipalities play a crucial role in establishing the necessary infrastructure for waste collection, sorting, and processing. This includes providing accessible and clearly labeled bins for different waste streams, ensuring regular collection services, and investing in advanced recycling and composting facilities.

Policy measures, such as regulations, incentives, and penalties, can drive the adoption of waste segregation practices. Regulations mandating the separation of waste at the source can ensure compliance and consistency across communities. Incentives, such as reduced waste disposal fees for segregated waste or rewards for recycling, can encourage individuals and businesses to participate in segregation efforts. Penalties for non-compliance can serve as a deterrent, reinforcing the importance of proper waste management.

Education and awareness are fundamental to the success of waste segregation initiatives. By informing individuals and communities about the importance and benefits of segregation, educational campaigns can foster a culture of responsibility and participation. These initiatives can include school programs, community workshops, and public awareness campaigns that provide practical guidance on waste segregation practices. Clear communication and consistent messaging are essential to ensure that individuals understand how to properly segregate waste and the positive impact of their actions.

Technology and innovation also have a role in enhancing waste segregation efforts. The development of smart waste management systems, such as sensor-equipped bins and data-driven collection services, can optimize waste collection and sorting processes. These technologies can improve efficiency, reduce contamination rates, and provide valuable data for waste management planning and policy development.

Community engagement and grassroots initiatives are vital for promoting waste segregation and building local capacity. Community-led projects, such as neighborhood recycling programs, composting initiatives, and waste reduction workshops, can inspire collective action and empower individuals to make a difference. By fostering a sense of ownership and collaboration, communities can create sustainable waste management systems tailored to their unique needs and contexts.

Overcoming the challenges of waste segregation requires collaboration and commitment from all stakeholders, including individuals, businesses, governments, and communities. By working together, we can develop and implement effective strategies that prioritize waste segregation and drive progress towards a more sustainable future.

Ultimately, the importance of waste segregation lies in its ability to transform waste from a problem into a resource. By embracing segregation practices, we can conserve resources, protect the environment, and create opportunities for sustainable development. Through education, innovation, and collaboration, waste segregation can become an integral part of our daily lives, ensuring a cleaner and healthier planet for generations to come.

Community Involvement in Waste Reduction

Community involvement stands as a cornerstone in the quest to achieve effective waste reduction. When individuals unite under a common goal, the collective impact can be profound, fostering not only a cleaner environment but also a strengthened community bond. Waste reduction is not merely about minimizing what we discard; it is an opportunity to rethink our lifestyle choices and foster a more sustainable future. By leveraging the power of community, we can drive significant change in waste management practices and inspire a cultural shift towards sustainability.

Imagine a neighborhood where every household takes part in waste reduction efforts. The transformation begins at the grassroots level, with neighbors coming together to discuss strategies for minimizing waste. These discussions often lead to the establishment of community-led initiatives, such as recycling cooperatives, communal composting projects, and local repair workshops. By sharing resources and knowledge, communities can create effective waste management systems tailored to their unique needs.

One of the most impactful ways communities can contribute to waste reduction is through organized recycling programs. By providing accessible and convenient recycling options, communities make it easier for individuals to participate. Local governments and organizations can collaborate to set up drop-off centers or curbside collection services, ensuring that recyclables are processed efficiently. Community events, such as recycling drives or educational workshops, can further promote recycling practices and increase awareness about the importance of diverting waste from landfills.

Composting is another powerful tool in the community waste reduction arsenal. Organic waste, such as food scraps and yard trimmings, makes up a significant portion of household waste. By composting these materials, communities can reduce the volume of waste sent to landfills, cutting down on methane emissions and producing nutrient-rich compost for local gardens. Community composting initiatives can take many forms, from shared compost bins in apartment complexes to large-scale municipal composting programs. These projects provide a valuable opportunity for community members to learn about the benefits of composting and actively participate in sustainable waste management.

Repair and reuse initiatives also play a crucial role in community waste reduction efforts. By promoting the repair of broken items and the reuse of materials, communities can extend the lifespan of products and reduce the demand for new resources. Repair cafes, where skilled volunteers help community members fix broken appliances, clothing, and other items, are gaining popularity as a way to reduce waste and foster community engagement. Similarly, swap events and thrift stores encourage the exchange and reuse of goods, promoting a circular economy that values sustainability over disposability.

Education and awareness are pivotal in engaging communities in waste reduction. By providing information about the environmental impact of waste and the benefits of sustainable practices, communities can empower individuals to make informed choices. Schools, community centers, and local organizations can offer workshops, seminars, and campaigns focused on waste reduction strategies. These initiatives can spark conversations, inspire action, and create a culture of sustainability that permeates the community.

Collaboration between different stakeholders is essential for the success of community-based waste reduction efforts. Local governments, businesses, non-profit organizations, and residents must work together to develop and implement effective strategies. Public-private partnerships can provide the resources and expertise needed to launch community waste reduction initiatives. By aligning goals and sharing responsibilities, stakeholders can create synergies that enhance the overall impact of waste reduction efforts.

Technology and innovation also have a role to play in community waste reduction. Digital platforms and applications can facilitate communication, coordination, and data collection, helping communities optimize waste management processes. For example, apps that track waste generation and diversion rates can provide valuable insights and motivate individuals to reduce their waste footprint. Additionally, technology can support the development of new waste reduction solutions, such as advanced recycling techniques or community energy projects that utilize organic waste.

While community involvement in waste reduction offers numerous benefits, it also presents challenges that must be addressed. Ensuring sustained engagement and participation can be difficult, particularly in diverse communities with varying priorities and resources. Effective communication, inclusive decision-making, and continuous support are essential to maintaining momentum and achieving long-term success. By fostering a sense of ownership and pride in waste reduction efforts, communities can overcome these challenges and inspire lasting change.

Ultimately, community involvement in waste reduction is about more than just managing waste—it's about building a sustainable future together. By working collaboratively, communities can create resilient systems that prioritize environmental stewardship, social equity, and economic vitality. Through shared efforts, we can transform waste into a resource, protect our planet for future generations, and strengthen the bonds that unite us.

Chapter 3: Reducing Waste at Home

Simple Changes for Daily Life

Embracing sustainability in daily life doesn't require sweeping changes or drastic sacrifices. Instead, it involves integrating simple, conscious choices that collectively make a significant impact on the environment. It's about understanding that small actions, when multiplied by millions of people, can lead to profound change. By adopting these simple changes, individuals can contribute to a more sustainable planet while enhancing their quality of life.

Consider the morning routine, a perfect starting point for introducing sustainable habits. Switching from single-use plastic bottles to a reusable water bottle reduces plastic waste and environmental pollution. This small change not only saves money but also decreases the demand for plastic production, which is energy-intensive and polluting. Similarly, opting for a reusable coffee cup instead of disposable ones can cut down on paper and plastic waste, as well as the resources used to produce them.

Energy consumption is another area where small adjustments can lead to substantial savings. Turning off lights when leaving a room, unplugging devices not in use, and using energy-efficient appliances are straightforward actions that reduce electricity usage. Installing LED bulbs can significantly decrease energy consumption and last longer than traditional incandescent bulbs, offering both environmental and economic benefits. Additionally, setting thermostats to a moderate temperature and using programmable thermostats can optimize heating and cooling, further reducing energy use.

Transportation choices also present opportunities for sustainable living. Walking or cycling for short trips not only reduces carbon emissions but also promotes physical health. For longer distances, using public transportation or carpooling can help decrease traffic congestion and lower greenhouse gas emissions. If driving is necessary, maintaining proper tire pressure and regular vehicle maintenance can improve fuel efficiency and reduce emissions. For those considering a new vehicle, exploring hybrid or electric options can further minimize environmental impact.

In the kitchen, food choices play a crucial role in sustainability. Reducing meat consumption, even slightly, can considerably lower one's carbon footprint, as meat production is resource-intensive and generates significant greenhouse gas emissions. Incorporating more plant-based meals into the diet is a delicious and nutritious way to support the environment. Additionally, buying local and seasonal produce supports local farmers, reduces transportation emissions, and often provides fresher, tastier options.

Minimizing food waste is another simple yet impactful change. Planning meals, making shopping lists, and storing food properly can prevent unnecessary waste. Leftovers can be repurposed into new meals, reducing the need to buy more ingredients. Composting food scraps is an effective way to recycle organic waste, returning nutrients to the soil and reducing landfill contributions. By being mindful of food consumption and waste, individuals can save money and resources while supporting a sustainable food system.

Personal care and household products offer further opportunities for sustainable choices. Selecting products with minimal packaging or those packaged in recyclable materials can reduce waste. Many companies now offer refillable options for soaps, shampoos, and cleaning products, minimizing single-use plastic. Choosing eco-friendly products made from natural ingredients can also reduce exposure to harmful chemicals and support environmentally responsible businesses.

Clothing and fashion choices are another area where small changes can make a big difference. Embracing a more minimalist wardrobe, purchasing high-quality, timeless pieces, and supporting sustainable fashion brands can reduce the environmental impact of clothing production. Buying second-hand or organizing clothing swaps with friends are great ways to refresh a wardrobe without contributing to fast fashion waste.

Technology use, while integral to modern life, can also be approached sustainably. Opting for digital subscriptions instead of physical copies for books, magazines, and newspapers can save paper and reduce waste. Properly recycling electronic devices and choosing to repair instead of replace can extend the life of gadgets and reduce e-waste. Being mindful of screen time and reducing unnecessary device use can also contribute to energy savings.

Incorporating a sustainable mindset into daily life extends beyond individual actions. It involves fostering a culture of sustainability within families and communities. Engaging in conversations about environmental issues, sharing tips and resources, and participating in community sustainability initiatives can amplify individual efforts and inspire collective action.

Educating children and young people about the importance of sustainability ensures that future generations are equipped with the knowledge and values needed to continue the journey toward a sustainable world. Encouraging them to participate in sustainable practices, such as recycling, gardening, or conserving water, instills lifelong habits and an appreciation for the environment.

Ultimately, living sustainably is about valuing quality over quantity, making thoughtful choices, and recognizing the interconnectedness of our actions and the natural world. By embracing simple changes in daily life, individuals can lead by example, inspiring others to join the movement toward a more sustainable and resilient future. These small, consistent actions not only contribute to the well-being of the planet but also enhance personal well-being, fostering a sense of purpose and connection to the larger global community.

Composting Basics

Composting is a natural process that transforms organic waste into nutrient-rich material, offering an effective way to recycle kitchen scraps and yard waste. By embracing composting, individuals can reduce household waste, enrich soil, and contribute to a more sustainable environment. Understanding the basics of composting can empower anyone to start this eco-friendly practice right in their backyard or even on a small apartment balcony.

At its core, composting involves the decomposition of organic materials by microorganisms, such as bacteria and fungi. These tiny organisms break down the waste into humus, a dark, crumbly substance rich in nutrients. The process mimics what happens in nature, where leaves, twigs, and other organic matter decompose on forest floors, enriching the soil.

To start composting, one must first choose a suitable location and method. For those with ample outdoor space, building a compost pile or using a compost bin are popular options. A compost pile is simply an open heap of organic material, while a bin provides more structure and can help contain the compost. For urban dwellers or those with limited space, worm composting, also known as vermicomposting, is a compact and efficient method. This technique uses worms to accelerate the decomposition process, allowing for composting indoors or in small areas.

Once the method is chosen, it's crucial to understand what materials can be composted. A successful compost pile requires a balanced mix of "greens" and "browns." Greens are nitrogen-rich materials, including fruit and vegetable scraps, coffee grounds, and grass clippings. Browns, on the other hand, are carbon-rich and include items like dried leaves, straw, and cardboard. This balance is essential because it provides the microorganisms with the energy and nutrients they need to thrive.

Avoid adding meat, dairy, or oily foods to the compost, as they can attract pests and create unpleasant odors. Similarly, diseased plants or weeds with mature seeds should be excluded to prevent spreading them when the compost is used. It's also wise to avoid composting glossy paper, treated wood, or synthetic materials, as they may contain chemicals that could harm the composting process.

Building the compost pile involves layering these materials to create an environment conducive to decomposition. A typical approach is to start with a layer of browns, followed by greens, and then repeat the layers until the pile reaches the desired height. Ensuring that each layer is moist, like a damp sponge, helps the microorganisms thrive. If the pile becomes too dry, adding water can help maintain the necessary moisture level.

Aeration is another critical component of composting. Oxygen is vital for the microorganisms responsible for decomposition. By regularly turning the compost pile or using a pitchfork to create air pockets, one can ensure sufficient airflow, speeding up the process and preventing unpleasant odors. For those using a compost bin, selecting a model with built-in ventilation or rotating it periodically can achieve the same effect.

As the composting process unfolds, the pile will heat up, a sign that decomposition is actively occurring. The internal temperature can reach up to 140 degrees Fahrenheit (60 degrees Celsius), which helps kill off pathogens and weed seeds. Monitoring the temperature with a compost thermometer can provide insights into the pile's health and indicate when turning or additional materials might be needed.

Patience is an essential virtue in composting, as the process can take anywhere from a few months to over a year, depending on factors like climate, materials, and management practices. Recognizing when compost is ready involves observing its texture and smell. Finished compost, often called "black gold," should be dark, crumbly, and earthy in scent. If any recognizable bits of material remain, additional time or turning may be required.

The benefits of composting extend far beyond waste reduction. The resulting compost is a valuable soil amendment, enriching garden beds, potted plants, and lawns. Its application improves soil structure, enhances moisture retention, and provides essential nutrients for plant growth. By using compost, gardeners can reduce or eliminate the need for chemical fertilizers, promoting a healthier and more balanced ecosystem.

Additionally, composting contributes to reducing greenhouse gas emissions. Organic waste in landfills decomposes anaerobically, releasing methane, a potent greenhouse gas. By diverting this waste through composting, methane emissions can be significantly reduced, contributing to climate change mitigation.

Education and community involvement can further amplify the benefits of composting. Schools, community gardens, and local organizations can offer workshops and resources to teach composting techniques, fostering a culture of sustainability. Sharing experiences and knowledge within the community encourages more people to start composting and reinforces the importance of responsible waste management.

For those who wish to take their composting efforts to the next level, experimenting with different materials, techniques, and systems can lead to new insights and improvements. Advanced composters might explore building hot compost piles for faster decomposition or creating specific compost blends tailored to certain plants or soil types.

Composting is more than a method of waste management; it's a transformative practice that connects individuals to the natural cycles of growth and decay. By adopting composting, individuals can contribute to a more sustainable future, enriching the earth while nurturing a deeper understanding of their role in the environment. With knowledge, patience, and commitment, anyone can master the art of composting and make a positive impact on the planet.

DIY Household Products

Creating your own household products is an empowering way to embrace sustainability while reducing reliance on commercial goods that often contain harsh chemicals and excessive packaging. By crafting your own cleaning supplies, personal care items, and other household necessities, you not only gain control over the ingredients used but also enjoy the satisfaction of producing something with your own hands. Whether you're motivated by environmental concerns, health considerations, or simply a desire to be more self-sufficient, these DIY solutions offer both practicality and creativity.

Start with cleaning products, as they offer some of the easiest and most impactful DIY opportunities. Many commercial cleaning agents are made with a cocktail of synthetic chemicals that can be harmful to both health and the environment. By using simple, natural ingredients, you can create effective alternatives that are just as potent without the negative side effects. White vinegar, for instance, serves as a powerful base for many DIY cleaners due to its antibacterial properties and ability to cut through grease. Mixing vinegar with water and a few drops of essential oil creates an all-purpose cleaner suitable for a variety of surfaces.

Baking soda is another versatile ingredient, often hailed for its ability to neutralize odors and act as a gentle abrasive. A paste made from baking soda and water can scrub away stubborn stains in sinks and bathtubs, while a sprinkle of baking soda in the trash bin or refrigerator helps keep unpleasant odors at bay. When combined with vinegar, baking soda can also unclog drains, offering a natural alternative to chemical-laden commercial drain cleaners.

For those who prefer scented cleaning products, essential oils provide an aromatic touch while offering additional cleaning benefits. Lemon, tea tree, and lavender oils are popular choices, known for their antimicrobial properties. Adding a few drops to homemade cleaners not only enhances their effectiveness but also leaves your home smelling fresh and inviting.

Beyond cleaning, personal care products are another area where DIY solutions shine. Many store-bought toiletries contain synthetic fragrances, preservatives, and other additives that can irritate sensitive skin. By making your own, you can tailor the ingredients to suit your preferences and needs. A simple body scrub, for example, can be made by mixing sugar or salt with coconut oil and a few drops of essential oil. This exfoliating blend gently removes dead skin cells, leaving your skin soft and moisturized.

Deodorant is another personal care product that lends itself well to a DIY approach. By combining coconut oil, baking soda, and arrowroot powder, you can create a natural deodorant that effectively combats odor without the use of aluminum or other potentially harmful chemicals. A few drops of your favorite essential oil can be added for fragrance, allowing you to customize the scent to your liking.

Shampoo and conditioner can also be crafted at home using natural ingredients. A basic shampoo can be made by mixing castile soap with water and essential oils, while a simple conditioner can be created by diluting apple cider vinegar with water. These DIY hair care products are gentle on both your hair and the environment, free from the sulfates and silicones often found in commercial brands.

Household air fresheners are another area where DIY solutions can provide a refreshing alternative. Many store-bought air fresheners mask odors with synthetic fragrances that can contribute to indoor air pollution. Instead, consider making your own by simmering a pot of water with natural ingredients like citrus peels, cinnamon sticks, and cloves. Alternatively, a spray bottle filled with water and a few drops of essential oils can serve as a simple and effective air freshener.

Laundry care can also benefit from DIY approaches. Homemade laundry detergent, made from washing soda, borax, and grated bar soap, cleans clothes effectively without the synthetic fragrances and dyes found in commercial detergents. For fabric softening, vinegar can be used in the rinse cycle, leaving clothes soft and fresh without the residue of traditional softeners.

The benefits of making DIY household products extend beyond health and environmental considerations. They also offer an opportunity for creativity and experimentation, allowing you to customize products to your liking. Additionally, DIY solutions are often more cost-effective than their store-bought counterparts, saving money in the long run.

Embracing DIY household products can also foster a sense of community and shared learning. Friends and neighbors can exchange recipes and tips, while workshops and social media groups provide platforms for sharing experiences and discoveries. This collective knowledge and support encourage more people to try their hand at DIY, spreading the message of sustainability and self-reliance.

For those new to DIY, starting with a few simple recipes can build confidence and lay the foundation for more advanced projects. It's important to remember that DIY doesn't mean sacrificing effectiveness or quality; rather, it offers a way to align your household practices with your values, making thoughtful choices about the products you use.

Incorporating DIY household products into daily life is a step towards greater independence and ecological responsibility. With a bit of creativity and a willingness to experiment, anyone can begin crafting their own solutions, reducing waste, and minimizing exposure to unwanted chemicals. These efforts, though small on an individual scale, contribute to a larger movement towards sustainable living, empowering individuals to take control of their environment and resources. Through DIY, we can transform our homes into havens of health and sustainability, reflecting a commitment to a more mindful way of living.

Eco-Friendly Shopping Habits

Navigating the world of consumerism with an eco-conscious mindset requires intentionality and awareness. Adopting eco-friendly shopping habits is more than just a trend—it's a lifestyle change that prioritizes the environment, supports ethical practices, and often leads to more meaningful consumption. By making thoughtful choices about what and how we buy, we can contribute to a more sustainable economy and reduce our environmental footprint.

The journey to eco-friendly shopping begins with understanding the impact of our purchases. Every product has a lifecycle, from raw material extraction to manufacturing, distribution, and disposal. This lifecycle affects the environment at every stage, consuming resources and generating waste. By considering this full lifecycle, shoppers can make informed decisions that minimize negative impacts and support sustainability.

One of the most effective ways to reduce environmental impact is to embrace the principle of "less is more." By prioritizing quality over quantity, consumers can select items that are durable, timeless, and versatile. Investing in fewer, higher-quality products reduces the frequency of replacement, ultimately decreasing waste and conserving resources. This approach also encourages a shift away from fast fashion and disposable goods, which are often produced under unsustainable and unethical conditions.

Informed consumers also pay attention to the materials used in the products they purchase. Opting for items made from sustainable, renewable, or recycled materials can significantly reduce environmental impact. For example, choosing clothing made from organic cotton, hemp, or Tencel minimizes pesticide use and water consumption compared to conventional cotton. Similarly, products made from recycled plastics or metals help reduce the demand for virgin materials and the energy-intensive processes required to produce them.

Labels and certifications can be valuable tools in identifying eco-friendly products. Certifications such as Fair Trade, USDA Organic, or Forest Stewardship Council (FSC) indicate that products meet specific environmental or ethical standards. These labels provide assurance that the products were produced with consideration for social and environmental responsibility. However, it's important for consumers to be aware of "greenwashing," where companies make misleading claims about the environmental benefits of their products. Educating oneself about reputable certifications can help navigate these claims.

Packaging is another critical aspect of eco-friendly shopping. The packaging often contributes significantly to environmental waste, with many products wrapped in excessive plastic or non-recyclable materials. Consumers can reduce waste by choosing products with minimal or recyclable packaging. Bringing reusable bags, containers, and produce sacks to the store is a simple yet effective way to cut down on single-use plastics. Additionally, buying in bulk can further reduce packaging waste and often saves money.

Supporting local and independent businesses can enhance eco-friendly shopping efforts. Local products typically require less transportation, reducing carbon emissions associated with long-distance shipping. Additionally, small businesses often have a more direct connection to their supply chains, allowing them to prioritize sustainable practices and ethical sourcing. By supporting these businesses, consumers can contribute to their local economies and promote sustainable community development.

Food shopping presents unique opportunities for eco-friendly practices. Opting for seasonal and locally-grown produce not only supports local farmers but also reduces the environmental impact of transportation and storage. Farmers' markets and community-supported agriculture (CSA) programs are excellent resources for accessing fresh, local foods. Reducing meat consumption, or choosing sustainably-raised animal products, can also significantly lower one's carbon footprint, as meat production is resource-intensive and generates substantial greenhouse gas emissions.

Online shopping, while convenient, poses its own set of challenges for eco-friendly consumers. The convenience of quick deliveries often comes with increased packaging waste and carbon emissions. To mitigate these impacts, consumers can consolidate orders to reduce shipping frequency, choose slower shipping options, and support online retailers that prioritize sustainable practices. Some companies offer carbon-neutral shipping or use recycled packaging materials, making them preferable choices for eco-conscious shoppers.

The concept of a circular economy—where products are designed for reuse, repair, and recycling—aligns closely with eco-friendly shopping habits. By embracing second-hand shopping, consumers can extend the lifecycle of products and reduce demand for new resources. Thrift stores, consignment shops, and online resale platforms offer a wide array of pre-owned goods, from clothing to electronics. This approach not only benefits the environment but also provides unique and affordable options for consumers.

Sustainable shopping is not solely about the products themselves but also about the habits surrounding consumption. Mindfulness and intentionality are key components of eco-friendly shopping. Before making a purchase, consumers can ask themselves if the item is truly necessary, if it will be used and appreciated, and if it aligns with their values. By practicing mindful consumption, individuals can reduce impulse buys, save money, and focus on acquiring items that enhance their lives and reflect their commitment to sustainability.

Education and advocacy are powerful tools for promoting eco-friendly shopping habits. By sharing knowledge and experiences with friends, family, and the broader community, individuals can inspire others to consider the environmental impact of their purchases. Supporting policies and initiatives that promote sustainable production, waste reduction, and ethical labor practices can also drive systemic change in the marketplace.

Ultimately, eco-friendly shopping habits are about making choices that reflect a commitment to the health of the planet and its inhabitants. By considering the broader implications of our consumption, we can make a positive impact on the environment, support ethical businesses, and cultivate a more sustainable future. The journey toward sustainable shopping is ongoing, requiring continuous learning and adaptation, but each mindful purchase is a step toward a more conscientious and connected world.

The Benefits of Minimalism

Minimalism is more than a design trend or a fleeting lifestyle choice; it's a deliberate shift in the way we approach our lives and the possessions we allow into them. At its core, minimalism is about focusing on what truly matters by removing the excess that distracts us from it. In a world increasingly cluttered with material goods and digital noise, embracing minimalism offers a path to clarity, purpose, and freedom.

Imagine walking into a room where every object serves a purpose or brings you joy. There's space to breathe, both physically and mentally. This is the essence of minimalism—creating an environment that supports, rather than hinders, our well-being.

By stripping away the nonessential, minimalism allows us to rediscover the value of simplicity and the peace that accompanies it.

One of the most immediate benefits of minimalism is the reduction of stress and anxiety. Cluttered spaces often lead to cluttered minds, where the constant visual noise can overwhelm and distract. By curating our surroundings and removing the unnecessary, we create a calming atmosphere that fosters focus and relaxation. This physical decluttering often translates into mental decluttering, helping individuals prioritize their thoughts and responsibilities more effectively.

Financial freedom is another compelling advantage of minimalism. By adopting a minimalist mindset, individuals become more mindful of their purchasing decisions, focusing on quality rather than quantity. This shift can lead to significant savings, as the impulse to buy is replaced by careful consideration of necessity and value. Over time, these savings can accumulate, providing financial security and the flexibility to pursue other interests or experiences.

Minimalism also encourages a deeper connection with the things we choose to keep. When possessions are no longer abundant, each item holds greater significance and purpose. This mindfulness extends to how we care for our belongings, promoting a culture of repair and maintenance over disposability. By valuing what we have, we reduce waste and contribute to a more sustainable lifestyle.

In the realm of personal growth, minimalism fosters self-awareness and introspection. By removing distractions, individuals are better able to focus on their values, goals, and passions. This clarity can lead to more intentional living, where decisions are guided by what truly matters rather than societal pressures or fleeting desires. Minimalism challenges us to define our own versions of success and happiness, independent of external influences.

The benefits of minimalism extend to our relationships as well. By prioritizing experiences over possessions, minimalists often find themselves with more time and energy to invest in connections with others. This shift from material accumulation to meaningful interactions can strengthen bonds and foster a sense of community. Minimalism encourages us to be present, to listen, and to engage fully with those around us.

Moreover, minimalism can serve as a catalyst for creativity and innovation. With fewer distractions and a clearer mind, individuals can channel their energy into creative pursuits, problem-solving, and personal development. The constraints of minimalism often inspire new ways of thinking, as limitations can foster ingenuity and resourcefulness.

Adopting a minimalist lifestyle doesn't mean sacrificing comfort or depriving oneself of joy. Rather, it's about finding contentment in simplicity and redefining luxury as the absence of excess. Minimalism is inherently flexible, allowing individuals to tailor its principles to their unique circumstances and preferences. Whether it's a complete lifestyle overhaul or small, incremental changes, the essence of minimalism is accessible to anyone willing to embrace it.

The journey toward minimalism often begins with a process of decluttering. This involves evaluating each possession and asking whether it adds value or joy to one's life. This practice can be both liberating and challenging, as it requires honesty and self-reflection. However, the rewards of a decluttered space and mind are well worth the effort.

Digital minimalism is another aspect of this lifestyle that addresses the pervasive influence of technology. By setting boundaries on screen time, curating digital content, and focusing on meaningful online interactions, individuals can reclaim control over their digital lives. This approach promotes a healthier relationship with technology, allowing for more intentional use and reducing the constant barrage of information and distractions.

Incorporating minimalism into daily routines can lead to a more balanced and fulfilling life. From simplifying wardrobe choices to streamlining meal planning, these practices reduce decision fatigue and free up time for more meaningful activities. Minimalism encourages us to savor life's simple pleasures, such as a walk in nature, a shared meal, or a quiet moment of reflection.

Ultimately, minimalism is about creating a life that aligns with one's values and aspirations. It's a journey of self-discovery and empowerment, where the focus shifts from accumulation to appreciation. By embracing minimalism, individuals can find greater peace, clarity, and purpose, leading to a richer and more intentional existence. Minimalism invites us to live with less, but experience more—more freedom, more joy, and more connection to ourselves and the world around us.

Chapter 4: Recycling and Reusing: A Deeper Dive

Understanding Recycling Symbols

Recycling is a cornerstone of sustainable living, but the effectiveness of recycling efforts often hinges on understanding the symbols associated with it. These symbols, typically found on packaging and products, offer guidance on how to properly dispose of materials and ensure they are processed correctly. Although they may seem like cryptic codes at first glance, familiarizing oneself with these symbols can significantly enhance recycling habits and contribute to a more sustainable lifestyle.

The most recognizable recycling symbol is the Mobius loop, a triangle formed by three chasing arrows. This icon signifies that a product is recyclable, meaning it can be collected, processed, and manufactured into new products. However, the presence of this symbol doesn't guarantee that the item is recyclable in every community. Local recycling capabilities vary, and it's crucial to check with local facilities to understand what materials they accept.

Within the Mobius loop, some products include a number or abbreviation that provides additional information about the type of material. These numbers range from 1 to 7 and correspond to different types of plastic, each with its own recycling process and reusability. Understanding these categories can help consumers make informed decisions about purchasing and disposing of plastic products.

Number 1, or PET (polyethylene terephthalate), is commonly found in beverage bottles and food containers. It's widely accepted by recycling programs and can be transformed into products like fleece clothing and carpeting. Number 2, or HDPE (high-density polyethylene), is used for items such as milk jugs and detergent bottles. This type of plastic is also readily recyclable and can be made into new bottles or piping.

Number 3, or PVC (polyvinyl chloride), is less commonly accepted for recycling due to the harmful chemicals it can release during processing. Found in products like plumbing pipes and vinyl flooring, PVC is best avoided when possible. Number 4, or LDPE (low-density polyethylene), is used in items like grocery bags and some food wraps. While not always accepted in curbside recycling, many stores offer drop-off programs for these materials.

Number 5, or PP (polypropylene), is found in products such as yogurt containers and bottle caps. Though not universally accepted, recycling programs are gradually expanding their capabilities to include PP. Number 6, or PS (polystyrene), is used in disposable cutlery and foam packaging. Its recycling is limited due to its lightweight nature and the cost of processing, so it's advisable to minimize its use.

Number 7 is a catch-all category for other plastics, including biodegradable and compostable plastics. These materials often require specialized facilities for processing and may not be suitable for conventional recycling streams. Understanding the limitations of these plastics can help consumers make more sustainable choices.

In addition to the Mobius loop and plastic codes, other symbols provide valuable information about a product's environmental impact. The Green Dot, for example, indicates that the manufacturer has contributed financially to the recycling of packaging in Europe. However, it doesn't mean the product is recyclable in all locales. Similarly, the Tidyman symbol, depicting a figure disposing of litter in a bin, serves as a reminder to dispose of waste responsibly, but it provides no information about recyclability.

Paper products often feature their own set of recycling symbols. The most common is the recycling logo accompanied by the word "Recyclable." It signifies that the paper can be processed into new paper products. Some products also display a percentage, indicating the amount of recycled content they contain. Choosing products with high recycled content supports the market for recycled materials and reduces the demand for virgin resources.

Glass and metal packaging are generally more straightforward to recycle. Glass bottles and jars, when free of food residue, are widely accepted by recycling programs and can be indefinitely recycled without loss of quality. Metal cans, made from aluminum or steel, are also highly recyclable and can be transformed into new cans or other metal products. The recycling of these materials conserves energy and resources, making them preferable choices for packaging.

Electronic waste, or e-waste, presents unique challenges due to its complex composition and potential hazardous materials. Proper disposal of electronics often requires taking them to designated e-waste recycling centers, where they can be safely dismantled and processed. Understanding recycling symbols specific to electronics, such as the crossed-out wheelie bin, can help consumers identify products that should not be disposed of with regular waste.

Beyond understanding symbols, effective recycling requires proactive involvement. Keeping recyclables clean and free of contaminants, such as food residue or non-recyclable materials, is essential for maintaining the integrity of the recycling stream. Mixing different materials, like plastic bags in paper recycling, can disrupt the recycling process and lead to entire batches being discarded.

Educating oneself about local recycling guidelines and staying informed about changes in recycling capabilities can further enhance recycling efforts. Many municipalities provide resources and information to help residents navigate their recycling programs. By participating in community education initiatives or advocating for improved recycling infrastructure, individuals can play a vital role in advancing sustainability efforts.

Understanding recycling symbols is not just about deciphering labels; it's about making informed choices that support a circular economy and reduce environmental impact. By recognizing the significance of these symbols and applying this knowledge to daily habits, consumers can contribute to a more efficient and effective recycling system. This awareness transforms the act of recycling from a routine task into a conscious effort to protect and preserve our planet for future generations.

Innovative Upcycling Ideas

Upcycling breathes new life into discarded items, transforming them into something both functional and beautiful. This creative process not only reduces waste but also encourages innovation and resourcefulness. By reimagining the potential of everyday objects, upcycling offers a sustainable solution to overconsumption and waste, turning what might otherwise be trash into treasure.

Consider an old wooden pallet, often seen as nothing more than a shipping byproduct. With a little imagination, it can become a rustic coffee table or a vertical garden for herbs and flowers. Sanding down the wood, applying a fresh coat of paint or varnish, and adding some wheels can transform this humble piece into a stylish and functional addition to any home. The joy of upcycling lies in its ability to turn something ordinary into a unique statement piece, infused with personality and character.

Glass jars, ubiquitous in kitchens everywhere, offer another perfect canvas for upcycling. Instead of tossing them into the recycling bin, they can be repurposed as chic storage solutions, candle holders, or even planters. Wrapping them in twine or painting them with vibrant colors can add a decorative touch, making them ideal for organizing small items or displaying fresh flowers. The versatility of glass jars demonstrates how upcycling can blend creativity with practicality, enhancing everyday life with little effort.

Textiles present a wealth of upcycling opportunities, particularly for those with a knack for sewing or crafting. Old t-shirts can be transformed into reusable shopping bags or braided rugs, while worn-out jeans can become stylish tote bags or even quilted throws. By repurposing fabric, you not only extend the life of the material but also create one-of-a-kind pieces that reflect your personal style. This approach reduces the demand for new textiles and minimizes the environmental impact of fast fashion.

Furniture, often seen as a major investment, can also benefit from the upcycling treatment. A tired, outdated chair can be revitalized with a fresh coat of paint and new upholstery, turning it into a vibrant focal point. An old dresser might find new life as a bathroom vanity with the addition of a sink and plumbing. The possibilities are endless, limited only by imagination and willingness to experiment. Upcycling furniture not only saves money but also allows for customization that mass-produced items can't offer.

Even small household items, often overlooked, can undergo remarkable transformations. Tin cans become pencil holders or lanterns with the addition of some paint and creativity. Wine corks, collected over time, can be fashioned into coasters, trivets, or even bulletin boards. These projects not only repurpose materials that might otherwise be discarded but also provide a sense of accomplishment and satisfaction that comes from crafting something by hand.

Electronics, a growing source of waste, present unique challenges and opportunities for upcycling. While not everyone has the skills to transform old gadgets into new devices, parts can be harvested for other projects. Circuit boards, for instance, can be turned into jewelry or art pieces, while components like LEDs and motors can be used in DIY electronics projects. Upcycling electronics requires a bit more technical know-how, but the rewards include reducing e-waste and learning valuable skills.

Upcycling extends beyond individual projects and can foster a sense of community and shared purpose. Workshops and upcycling events bring people together to exchange ideas, materials, and skills, creating a collaborative atmosphere where creativity thrives. By participating in these activities, individuals can learn from one another, drawing inspiration from different perspectives and techniques.

The benefits of upcycling are not limited to environmental impact and personal satisfaction. It also promotes a mindset of resourcefulness and innovation, encouraging individuals to see potential where others see waste. This shift in perspective can lead to a more sustainable approach to consumption, where items are valued for their utility and potential rather than their novelty.

For those new to upcycling, the process can be both exciting and daunting. Starting with simple projects, such as repurposing glass jars or tin cans, can build confidence and inspire more ambitious endeavors. It's important to approach upcycling with a spirit of experimentation and a willingness to embrace imperfections. After all, the beauty of upcycling lies In Its unIqueness—the ability to create something that is truly one-of-a-kind.

Innovation in upcycling is driven by a combination of creativity, necessity, and environmental consciousness. As resources become scarcer and the consequences of waste more apparent, upcycling offers a practical and imaginative solution. By looking at the world through the lens of possibility, we can redefine waste as a resource and contribute to a more sustainable future.

Upcycling invites us to reimagine our relationship with objects, shifting from a disposable mindset to one of appreciation and ingenuity. Each upcycled creation tells a story, reflecting the history of its materials and the vision of its creator. This narrative adds depth and meaning to our surroundings, enriching our lives and encouraging us to think differently about consumption and sustainability. Through upcycling, we can transform not only objects but also our understanding of what it means to live sustainably and creatively in a world of finite resources.

The Economics of Recycling

Recycling is often viewed through the lens of environmental stewardship, but its economic implications are equally significant. The economics of recycling encompass a complex interplay of costs, savings, market dynamics, and policy frameworks. Understanding these elements reveals how recycling contributes to both local and global economies, while also highlighting the challenges and opportunities that define its economic landscape.

At the heart of recycling economics is the concept of resource efficiency. By recovering materials from waste, recycling reduces the need for virgin resources, which are often more costly to extract and process. This reduction in resource extraction can lead to substantial economic savings, as it decreases the energy and labor required in the initial stages of production. For instance, recycling aluminum saves up to 95% of the energy needed to produce new aluminum from bauxite ore. These savings translate into lower production costs for manufacturers and, ultimately, lower prices for consumers.

The recycling industry itself is a significant contributor to the economy, providing jobs and generating revenue. The process of collecting, sorting, and processing recyclables requires a workforce at every stage, from waste management professionals to factory workers who convert recycled materials into new products. According to industry reports, recycling and reuse activities in the United States alone support hundreds of thousands of jobs and billions of dollars in annual revenue. This economic activity not only supports livelihoods but also stimulates growth in related sectors, such as transportation and manufacturing.

Furthermore, recycling creates opportunities for innovation and entrepreneurship. As companies seek to improve recycling technologies and processes, they drive advancements that can enhance efficiency and profitability. Innovations in recycling, such as advanced sorting technologies and chemical recycling methods, not only reduce operational costs but also open new markets for recycled materials. Entrepreneurs can capitalize on these developments by creating businesses that specialize in innovative recycling solutions or by developing products that incorporate recycled content.

However, the economics of recycling are not without their challenges. One significant issue is the volatility of recycled material markets. Prices for recyclables can fluctuate based on factors such as global demand, commodity prices, and changes in trade policies. For example, a surge in demand for recycled paper in one region can drive up prices, while a decline in demand for recycled plastics in another can cause prices to plummet. This volatility can make it difficult for recycling businesses to plan and invest with confidence.

Policy and regulation also play critical roles in shaping the economics of recycling. Governments can influence recycling through incentives, mandates, and infrastructure investments. Policies such as extended producer responsibility (EPR) require manufacturers to take responsibility for the end-of-life management of their products, encouraging them to design for recyclability and invest in recycling programs. Similarly, deposit return schemes for beverage containers incentivize consumers to recycle by providing monetary returns for returned bottles and cans. These policies can drive higher recycling rates and create stable markets for recyclables.

On a local level, municipalities face the economic challenge of managing recycling programs efficiently. The costs associated with collection, sorting, and processing can strain municipal budgets, especially when market prices for recyclables are low. To address these challenges, some communities have turned to public-private partnerships, where private companies manage recycling operations while municipalities provide oversight and support. These collaborations can bring expertise, innovation, and investment to local recycling efforts, enhancing their economic viability.

Recycling also intersects with broader economic trends, such as the circular economy. A circular economy seeks to minimize waste and maximize resource use by creating closed-loop systems where materials are continuously reused and recycled. This approach contrasts with the traditional linear economy, which follows a "take, make, dispose" model. By embracing circular economy principles, industries can reduce their environmental impact while unlocking new economic opportunities. Recycling is a foundational component of this model, facilitating the continuous flow of materials through the economy.

Consumer behavior is another economic factor that influences recycling. As consumers become more environmentally conscious, demand for products with recycled content increases. This shift creates market incentives for companies to incorporate recycled materials into their products and to invest in recycling infrastructure. By choosing products made from recycled materials, consumers can drive demand and support the economic viability of recycling.

Education and awareness initiatives can further enhance the economics of recycling by encouraging higher participation rates and reducing contamination. Contamination occurs when non-recyclable materials are mixed with recyclables, which can increase processing costs and reduce the quality of recycled materials. By educating the public about proper recycling practices, communities can improve the efficiency and effectiveness of their recycling programs, ultimately leading to better economic outcomes.

The economics of recycling are a dynamic and multifaceted domain, shaped by a range of factors from global markets to local policies. While challenges such as market volatility and contamination persist, the potential economic benefits of recycling are significant. By reducing resource costs, creating jobs, and fostering innovation, recycling contributes to a more sustainable and resilient economy. As societies continue to prioritize sustainability, the economic role of recycling will likely expand, offering new opportunities for growth and development in a world where resource conservation is increasingly paramount.

Challenges in the Recycling Industry

The recycling industry, while fundamental to sustainable waste management, faces numerous challenges that complicate its operations and objectives. These challenges range from economic fluctuations and technological limitations to consumer behavior and policy discrepancies. Understanding these obstacles is crucial for improving the efficiency and effectiveness of recycling systems worldwide.

One of the primary challenges facing the recycling industry is market volatility. The value of recycled materials is subject to fluctuations based on global demand, commodity prices, and economic conditions. For instance, when the price of virgin materials drops, manufacturers may opt for these cheaper alternatives over recycled ones, reducing demand for recyclables. This volatility can make it difficult for recycling facilities to remain financially viable, as their revenue is closely tied to the market value of the materials they process.

Contamination is another significant issue that affects the quality and value of recycled materials. When non-recyclable items are mixed with recyclables, they can spoil entire batches, increasing processing costs and reducing the marketability of the end product. Common contaminants include food waste, plastic bags, and incorrect materials placed in recycling bins. Overcoming contamination requires extensive public education and awareness campaigns to ensure consumers are informed about what can and cannot be recycled.

The recycling industry also grapples with technological limitations. While advancements have been made in sorting and processing technologies, many facilities still rely on outdated systems that struggle to efficiently separate and process complex materials. For example, multi-layer packaging, which combines different types of materials, poses a significant challenge for recycling facilities. Innovations in recycling technology are essential to improve the sorting process, reduce contamination, and increase the range of materials that can be recycled.

Logistical challenges further complicate recycling operations. The collection, transportation, and sorting of recyclables require substantial infrastructure and coordination. In regions with limited access to recycling facilities or inadequate infrastructure, the cost and complexity of transporting materials can be prohibitive. These logistical hurdles can lead to inefficiencies and increased greenhouse gas emissions, undermining the environmental benefits of recycling.

Policy and regulatory inconsistencies also pose challenges to the recycling industry. While some regions have robust recycling policies and infrastructure, others lack comprehensive regulations or enforcement mechanisms. This disparity can create confusion among consumers and businesses, hindering participation and compliance. Furthermore, international policies, such as import restrictions on recyclables, can impact global recycling markets. For instance, China's National Sword policy, which imposed strict contamination limits on imported recyclables, disrupted global recycling flows and forced many countries to reevaluate their recycling strategies.

Consumer behavior and participation significantly influence the success of recycling programs. Despite widespread awareness of recycling's importance, participation rates vary, and many consumers remain unsure about proper recycling practices. This uncertainty can lead to "wishcycling," where individuals place non-recyclable items in recycling bins in the hope they will be recycled. Enhancing consumer education and engagement is critical to overcoming these behavioral challenges and improving recycling outcomes.

The economics of recycling are further complicated by the costs associated with collection and processing, which can exceed the revenue generated from selling recycled materials. Municipalities often bear the financial burden of recycling programs, making it challenging to allocate resources for necessary improvements or expansions. Public-private partnerships and innovative funding models may offer solutions by sharing costs and leveraging private sector expertise.

The recycling industry also faces the challenge of adapting to changing waste streams. As consumer preferences and product designs evolve, so too do the types of materials entering the recycling system. The rise of e-commerce, for example, has led to an increase in packaging waste, while the proliferation of electronic devices has contributed to a growing e-waste problem. Recycling facilities must continuously adapt to these shifts to effectively manage and process diverse waste streams.

E-waste, in particular, presents unique challenges due to its complex composition and potential hazardous materials. Properly recycling electronics requires specialized facilities and processes to safely dismantle and recover valuable components. However, many regions lack the necessary infrastructure or regulations to manage e-waste effectively, leading to environmental and health risks from improper disposal.

Despite these challenges, the recycling industry holds significant potential for innovation and improvement. Embracing new technologies, such as artificial intelligence and robotics, can enhance sorting efficiency and reduce contamination. Developing standardized recycling labels and packaging designs can simplify consumer participation and improve material recovery. Additionally, fostering collaboration between governments, businesses, and communities can drive policy advancements and create more resilient recycling systems.

Addressing the challenges in the recycling industry requires a multifaceted approach that considers economic, technological, and social factors. By investing in infrastructure, education, and innovation, stakeholders can enhance the effectiveness of recycling programs and contribute to a more sustainable future. As the industry continues to evolve, it must remain adaptable and responsive to emerging trends and challenges, ensuring that recycling remains a vital component of global sustainability efforts.

How to Support Local Recycling Initiatives

Supporting local recycling initiatives is a powerful way to contribute to sustainability and environmental conservation. These initiatives often depend on community involvement and awareness to thrive, and by actively participating, individuals can help drive meaningful change. Whether through personal actions, community engagement, or advocacy, there are various ways to bolster local recycling efforts and ensure they succeed.

One of the most straightforward methods to support recycling initiatives is by becoming an informed participant. Understanding local recycling guidelines is crucial, as these can vary significantly between regions. By learning what materials are accepted, how they should be prepared, and what the collection schedule is, you can ensure that your recyclables are processed correctly. This knowledge helps reduce contamination, which is a major hurdle in recycling programs, and ensures that materials are as valuable and usable as possible.

Once you're familiar with the guidelines, sharing this knowledge with others can amplify your impact. Educating friends, family, and neighbors about proper recycling practices can increase participation rates and improve overall community compliance. Hosting informational sessions or workshops, whether in person or online, can be an effective way to spread awareness and provide hands-on guidance. By fostering a community culture of recycling, you help reinforce positive habits and encourage others to join the effort.

Volunteering with local recycling organizations or initiatives is another impactful way to contribute. Many recycling programs rely on volunteers to assist with activities such as sorting materials, organizing events, or conducting outreach. By offering your time and skills, you can help these programs run more smoothly and effectively. Volunteering not only supports the initiative directly but also provides an opportunity to learn more about the recycling process and connect with like-minded individuals.

Community events, such as recycling drives or clean-up days, offer additional opportunities to get involved. These events often require coordination and manpower to collect recyclables, sort materials, and educate participants. By helping organize or participate in these events, you can make recycling accessible and engaging for everyone. Additionally, events that combine recycling with other activities, such as workshops or educational talks, can attract a broader audience and increase community engagement.

Advocacy plays a crucial role in supporting local recycling initiatives. By advocating for stronger recycling policies and infrastructure, you can influence decision-makers to prioritize sustainability efforts. Writing to local representatives, attending city council meetings, or joining environmental advocacy groups can amplify your voice and help shape the future of local recycling programs. Advocacy efforts can lead to improved recycling facilities, increased funding, and the implementation of policies that encourage waste reduction and resource conservation.

Supporting local businesses that prioritize sustainability and recycling is another way to contribute. By choosing products and services from companies that use recycled materials or have robust recycling practices, you help create demand for sustainable business practices. Encouraging businesses to adopt recycling programs in their operations, whether through direct communication or by supporting policies that incentivize sustainable practices, can have a significant impact on local recycling efforts.

Educational institutions, such as schools and universities, are excellent platforms for promoting recycling initiatives. Engaging with these institutions to implement or enhance recycling programs can foster a culture of sustainability among students and staff. Organizing educational campaigns, recycling competitions, or sustainability workshops can inspire the next generation to be mindful of their environmental impact and take active roles in recycling efforts.

Innovative approaches to supporting recycling initiatives involve leveraging technology and social media. Social media platforms can be powerful tools for spreading awareness, organizing events, and mobilizing community action. Creating or participating in online groups dedicated to local recycling can facilitate information sharing and community building. Additionally, using technology to track recycling progress or reward participation can incentivize individuals to stay engaged and committed to their recycling goals.

For those interested in a more entrepreneurial approach, starting a local recycling project or business can be a rewarding way to support recycling initiatives. This could involve creating a service that collects hard-to-recycle items, developing products from recycled materials, or providing educational resources to the community. By identifying gaps in the local recycling system and addressing them through innovative solutions, you can contribute to a more robust and effective recycling infrastructure.

Finally, supporting local recycling initiatives requires a commitment to continuous learning and adaptation. Recycling practices and technologies are constantly evolving, and staying informed about new developments can help you support these initiatives more effectively. Attending workshops, reading up-to-date materials, and networking with other sustainability advocates can keep you informed and inspired.

Supporting local recycling initiatives is an ongoing journey that requires dedication, collaboration, and creativity. By participating in and advocating for recycling efforts, individuals can make a tangible difference in their communities and contribute to a more sustainable world. Through education, volunteerism, advocacy, and entrepreneurial innovation, everyone has the power to support and strengthen local recycling programs. In doing so, we collectively pave the way for a future where resources are conserved, waste is minimized, and communities thrive.

Chapter 5: Waste Management in Urban Environments

The Challenges of Urban Waste

The rapid urbanization of the modern world has brought with it a host of challenges, not least of which is the management of urban waste. As cities grow, so too does the volume of waste they produce, presenting complex issues that require innovative solutions. The challenges of urban waste encompass collection, processing, disposal, and the environmental impacts that arise from improper waste management. Understanding these challenges is crucial for developing effective strategies that ensure urban environments remain livable and sustainable.

One of the primary challenges in managing urban waste is the sheer volume generated by densely populated areas. Cities are home to a significant portion of the global population, and the concentration of people leads to increased production of municipal solid waste. This waste includes everything from household garbage to commercial refuse and construction debris. As cities expand, the infrastructure required to collect and process this waste often struggles to keep pace, leading to inefficiencies and service gaps.

The diversity of waste streams in urban areas further complicates waste management efforts. Urban waste is not limited to organic or inorganic categories but encompasses a wide range of materials, including plastics, metals, paper, electronics, and hazardous substances. Each type of waste requires specific handling and processing techniques, which can strain existing infrastructure and resources. For instance, electronic waste (e-waste) contains valuable metals but also toxic components that require specialized recycling facilities. The complexity of managing such diverse waste streams necessitates coordinated efforts and specialized knowledge.

In many cities, informal waste management systems coexist with formal municipal services. Informal waste workers, often operating without regulatory oversight or protection, play a vital role in collecting and recycling materials that might otherwise end up in landfills or the environment. While these workers contribute to waste reduction and recycling efforts, they face significant challenges, including unsafe working conditions and limited access to resources. Integrating informal waste management into formal systems can enhance efficiency and improve outcomes for both workers and the community.

Another challenge in urban waste management is the environmental impact of disposal practices. Landfills, the most common method of waste disposal, pose significant environmental risks, including leachate contamination of soil and groundwater, and the emission of methane, a potent greenhouse gas. Incineration, another common disposal method, can release harmful pollutants into the air if not properly managed. These environmental concerns underscore the need for sustainable waste management practices that prioritize reduction, reuse, and recycling over disposal.

Public participation and behavior play critical roles in the success of urban waste management systems. Despite widespread awareness of the importance of waste reduction and recycling, many urban residents remain disengaged or misinformed about proper waste disposal practices. This can lead to contamination of recyclables, illegal dumping, and other behaviors that undermine waste management efforts. Encouraging public participation through education and incentives is essential for creating a culture of sustainability and improving waste management outcomes.

The economic costs associated with urban waste management are another significant challenge. Collecting, transporting, and processing waste requires substantial financial investment, and cities often struggle to allocate sufficient resources to maintain and improve waste management infrastructure. Budget constraints can lead to service cutbacks, reduced collection frequency, and delayed infrastructure upgrades, all of which exacerbate waste management challenges. Innovative financing mechanisms, public-private partnerships, and policy incentives can help address these economic barriers.

Technological advancements offer promising solutions to the challenges of urban waste management, but their implementation is not without obstacles. New technologies, such as smart waste bins, automated sorting systems, and waste-to-energy processes, can enhance efficiency and reduce environmental impact. However, integrating these technologies into existing systems can be costly and require significant changes to infrastructure and operations. Additionally, technological solutions must be tailored to the specific needs and conditions of each urban area to be effective.

Urban planning and design also play crucial roles in addressing waste management challenges. Incorporating waste management considerations into city planning can lead to more efficient systems and reduced waste generation. For example, designing neighborhoods with convenient access to recycling facilities and composting sites can encourage residents to participate in waste reduction efforts. Similarly, implementing policies that promote sustainable construction practices can reduce the amount of construction and demolition waste generated as cities expand.

Collaboration among stakeholders is essential for overcoming the challenges of urban waste management. City governments, waste management companies, community organizations, and residents all have roles to play in creating effective waste management systems. By working together, these stakeholders can develop comprehensive strategies that address the unique challenges of their urban environments. Collaborative efforts can lead to the sharing of resources, knowledge, and best practices, ultimately resulting in more sustainable and efficient waste management solutions.

Education and awareness initiatives are critical components of any strategy to address urban waste challenges. By informing residents about the impacts of waste and the importance of proper disposal practices, cities can foster a sense of responsibility and engagement among the public. Educational campaigns can take many forms, from school programs and public workshops to social media campaigns and community events. By reaching diverse audiences and addressing common misconceptions, these initiatives can drive positive behavior change and support waste reduction efforts.

The challenges of urban waste are multifaceted and require holistic approaches that consider environmental, economic, social, and technological dimensions. While these challenges are significant, they also present opportunities for innovation and improvement. By implementing sustainable waste management practices, investing in technology, and fostering community engagement, urban areas can reduce their environmental impact and enhance the quality of life for their residents. As cities continue to grow and evolve, addressing the challenges of urban waste will be key to creating resilient and sustainable urban environments for future generations.

Implementing City-Wide Recycling Programs

Implementing city-wide recycling programs presents a formidable yet rewarding challenge for urban planners, policymakers, and community leaders. As cities grow and evolve, the need for efficient waste management becomes increasingly critical. Recycling programs, when effectively implemented, can significantly reduce waste sent to landfills, conserve natural resources, and foster a culture of sustainability among residents. To achieve these goals, cities must consider a comprehensive approach that encompasses education, infrastructure, policy, and community engagement.

The foundation of any successful recycling program is a robust infrastructure that supports the collection, processing, and marketing of recyclable materials. Establishing an efficient collection system is paramount, requiring the strategic placement of recycling bins and the integration of collection services with existing waste management operations. Cities must assess the logistical aspects of collection, including frequency, routes, and the types of materials accepted. By optimizing these elements, municipalities can create a system that is both cost-effective and convenient for residents.

Processing facilities play a crucial role in the recycling chain, transforming collected materials into marketable commodities.

Cities must invest in modern facilities equipped with advanced sorting technologies that can handle diverse waste streams. These technologies, such as optical sorters and magnetic separators, increase the efficiency and accuracy of material recovery, reducing contamination and improving the quality of recyclables. Collaboration with private sector partners can provide valuable expertise and resources to enhance processing capabilities.

A critical component of implementing a city-wide recycling program is developing a comprehensive public education campaign. Educating residents about the benefits of recycling and proper sorting practices is essential for maximizing participation and minimizing contamination. Public campaigns should utilize a variety of communication channels, including social media, community workshops, school programs, and informational materials. By tailoring messages to different demographics and addressing common misconceptions, cities can foster a culture of recycling and encourage residents to take an active role in waste reduction.

Incentive programs can further motivate residents to participate in recycling efforts. Offering rewards or recognition for households or neighborhoods with high recycling rates can create friendly competition and increase engagement. Pay-as-you-throw programs, where residents are charged based on the amount of waste they generate, can also incentivize waste reduction and recycling. By aligning financial incentives with environmental goals, cities can drive behavior change and reduce the overall waste footprint.

Policy development is another crucial aspect of implementing city-wide recycling programs. Municipalities must enact policies that support recycling efforts and create a framework for sustainable waste management. This includes setting recycling targets, establishing standards for recyclable materials, and implementing regulations that require businesses and institutions to participate in recycling. Policies should also address the management of specific waste streams, such as electronics or hazardous materials, to ensure proper disposal and recovery.

Collaboration with local businesses and industries is vital for the success of recycling programs. By engaging with stakeholders, cities can encourage businesses to adopt sustainable practices and integrate recycling into their operations. Public-private partnerships can facilitate the development of recycling infrastructure and create opportunities for innovative solutions. For example, businesses can collaborate with municipalities to establish take-back programs or sponsor community recycling events.

Monitoring and evaluation are essential components of any recycling program, providing insights into program performance and areas for improvement. Cities should establish metrics to assess the effectiveness of their recycling efforts, such as participation rates, contamination levels, and the volume of materials collected. Regular audits and feedback mechanisms can help identify challenges and inform adjustments to program design and implementation. By continuously monitoring progress, cities can adapt to changing conditions and ensure the long-term success of their recycling initiatives.

Community engagement is a cornerstone of effective recycling programs, emphasizing the importance of involving residents in decision-making processes. Establishing advisory committees or focus groups can provide valuable input and foster a sense of ownership among community members. By involving stakeholders in the planning and implementation phases, cities can create programs that reflect the needs and preferences of their residents, increasing buy-in and participation.

Equity considerations must also be addressed when implementing city-wide recycling programs. Ensuring that all residents have access to recycling services, regardless of socioeconomic status or geographic location, is essential for creating an inclusive and equitable system. Cities should prioritize outreach and support for underserved communities, providing resources and education to overcome barriers to participation. By addressing equity, municipalities can ensure that the benefits of recycling are shared by all residents.

The integration of technology can enhance the efficiency and effectiveness of recycling programs. Smart waste management systems, which use sensors and data analytics, can optimize collection routes, monitor bin fill levels, and identify contamination issues in real-time. Mobile applications and online platforms can facilitate communication between residents and waste management authorities, providing information on recycling guidelines and collection schedules. By leveraging technology, cities can improve service delivery and engage residents more effectively.

Implementing city-wide recycling programs is a complex undertaking that requires strategic planning, collaboration, and innovation. By building a strong infrastructure, engaging the public, developing supportive policies, and fostering partnerships, cities can create recycling programs that are both effective and sustainable. As urban populations continue to grow, the success of these programs will be instrumental in reducing waste, conserving resources, and promoting environmental stewardship for future generations.

Smart City Solutions for Waste Reduction

Urban centers across the globe are increasingly embracing the concept of smart city solutions to tackle the pressing issue of waste reduction. As populations surge, the strain on waste management systems intensifies, necessitating innovative approaches that leverage technology and data-driven insights. Smart city solutions offer a pathway to not only reduce waste but also optimize resources and enhance the quality of urban life. By exploring various technological advancements and strategies, cities can transform their waste management practices into efficient, sustainable systems.

One of the cornerstones of smart city waste management is the implementation of smart bins. These advanced waste receptacles are equipped with sensors that monitor the fill levels in real time. The data collected allows waste management authorities to optimize collection routes, ensuring that bins are emptied only when necessary, thereby reducing fuel consumption and operational costs. Additionally, smart bins can alert authorities to issues such as overflowing or illegal dumping, enabling prompt responses and maintaining cleanliness in public spaces.

The integration of data analytics is another powerful tool in the smart city arsenal. By analyzing patterns and trends in waste generation, cities can tailor their waste management strategies to specific needs and challenges. For instance, data can reveal peak waste generation times or areas with high contamination rates, allowing for targeted interventions. This data-driven approach enables cities to allocate resources more effectively and design waste reduction initiatives that resonate with community behaviors and preferences.

Technological advancements have also paved the way for innovative recycling solutions. Automated sorting systems, utilizing technologies such as artificial vision and robotics, can efficiently separate recyclables from waste streams, reducing contamination and improving the quality of recycled materials. These systems not only enhance the efficiency of recycling facilities but also increase the range of materials that can be processed, supporting circular economy principles.

Public engagement is an essential component of smart city waste reduction efforts. Mobile applications and online platforms can facilitate communication between residents and waste management authorities, providing information on recycling guidelines, collection schedules, and waste reduction tips. These platforms can also serve as channels for reporting issues such as missed collections or illegal dumping, fostering a sense of community involvement and accountability.

Gamification is an innovative strategy to encourage public participation in waste reduction. By incorporating elements of game design into environmental initiatives, cities can motivate residents to engage in sustainable behaviors. For example, a city might implement a points-based system where residents earn rewards for recycling correctly or reducing their waste output. This approach not only incentivizes positive behavior but also raises awareness about the impact of individual actions on the environment.

Collaboration between municipalities and the private sector is pivotal in driving smart city waste solutions. Public-private partnerships can accelerate the adoption of new technologies and bring expertise and resources to waste management initiatives. Businesses can play a role by adopting sustainable practices, such as reducing packaging waste or implementing take-back programs for products at the end of their lifecycle. These partnerships can lead to innovative solutions that benefit both the city and its residents.

Incorporating waste reduction into urban planning and design is another avenue for smart cities. Designing neighborhoods with convenient access to recycling and composting facilities can encourage residents to participate in waste reduction efforts. Policies that promote green building practices, such as using sustainable materials or incorporating waste-reduction technologies, can further support these goals. By integrating waste management considerations into the urban fabric, cities can create environments that naturally support sustainable behaviors.

The rise of the sharing economy presents additional opportunities for waste reduction in smart cities. Platforms that facilitate the sharing or reuse of goods, such as clothing, furniture, or electronics, can reduce the demand for new products and minimize waste generation. Supporting local initiatives that promote repair and refurbishment, such as tool libraries or repair cafes, can extend the lifespan of products and reduce the amount of waste sent to landfills.

Educational initiatives are critical to the success of smart city waste solutions. By raising awareness about the environmental and economic benefits of waste reduction, cities can foster a culture of sustainability among residents. Educational campaigns can target schools, businesses, and community groups, providing practical guidance on how to reduce waste and participate in recycling programs. By fostering a shared commitment to sustainability, cities can drive collective action and achieve significant waste reduction outcomes.

As cities continue to evolve, the importance of smart city solutions for waste reduction becomes increasingly apparent. By leveraging technology, data, and community engagement, cities can transform their waste management practices into efficient, sustainable systems that reduce environmental impact and enhance quality of life. While the challenges are significant, the potential benefits of smart city solutions are immense, offering a path toward a more sustainable and resilient urban future. Through innovation, collaboration, and education, cities can pave the way for a new era of waste management that prioritizes sustainability and resource conservation.

Case Studies of Successful Urban Waste Management

In the bustling heart of Copenhagen, a city known for its commitment to sustainability, the Amager Bakke waste-to-energy plant stands as a beacon of innovation in urban waste management. This facility, also known as CopenHill, is not only an architectural marvel but also a testament to Copenhagen's ambitious approach to reducing landfill waste and maximizing resource recovery. By transforming household waste into energy, the plant supplies electricity and heating to thousands of homes, demonstrating how urban centers can integrate waste management into broader sustainability goals.

Copenhagen's success with Amager Bakke is rooted in its holistic approach to waste. The city has implemented strict waste separation policies, encouraging residents to sort recyclables and compostables from general waste. This separation enhances the efficiency of the waste-to-energy process and reduces the volume of waste sent to the plant. Additionally, the plant's innovative design includes a rooftop ski slope and recreational facilities, seamlessly blending utility with leisure and engaging the community in the city's sustainability narrative.

Across the Atlantic, San Francisco has emerged as a leader in urban waste management through its Zero Waste by 2020 initiative. Driven by ambitious targets, the city has developed a comprehensive waste management strategy that emphasizes recycling, composting, and public education. San Francisco's mandatory recycling and composting ordinance, one of the first in the nation, requires residents and businesses to separate recyclables and compostables from trash. This policy has significantly increased diversion rates and reduced landfill contributions.

San Francisco's success is also attributed to its robust public outreach and education programs. The city has invested in campaigns that inform residents about proper waste sorting practices and the benefits of recycling and composting. By fostering a culture of environmental responsibility, San Francisco has empowered its citizens to actively participate in waste reduction efforts. The city's collaboration with waste haulers and recyclers has further strengthened its waste management infrastructure, ensuring efficient collection and processing of materials.

In Japan, the city of Kamikatsu has taken an extraordinary approach to waste management, striving to become the country's first zero-waste town. With limited access to landfill space, Kamikatsu has implemented an extensive waste separation system, requiring residents to sort their waste into 45 distinct categories. This meticulous sorting ensures that materials are appropriately recycled, composted, or reused, minimizing environmental impact and conserving resources.

Kamikatsu's commitment to zero waste extends beyond waste separation. The town actively promotes reuse and repair through community initiatives such as the Kuru Kuru Shop, where residents can exchange used items, and the Kuru Kuru Factory, which repurposes discarded textiles into new products. These efforts have cultivated a strong sense of community involvement and environmental stewardship, positioning Kamikatsu as a model for sustainable waste management.

In South Korea, Seoul has implemented a Pay-As-You-Throw (PAYT) system that has revolutionized its approach to waste management. Under this system, residents are charged for waste disposal based on the volume of waste they generate, incentivizing waste reduction and proper sorting. The PAYT program has led to significant decreases in landfill waste and increased recycling rates, demonstrating the effectiveness of economic incentives in driving behavioral change.

Seoul's success with the PAYT system is complemented by its investment in advanced recycling facilities and waste-to-energy plants. These facilities enhance the city's capacity to process recyclables and convert waste into energy, supporting its sustainability goals. Public engagement and education are integral components of Seoul's strategy, ensuring that residents understand the importance of waste reduction and recycling in achieving a sustainable urban environment.

In Europe, the city of Ljubljana, Slovenia, has garnered attention for its comprehensive waste management program that has positioned it as a leader in waste reduction. Ljubljana's strategy emphasizes waste prevention, recycling, and community involvement, resulting in one of the highest recycling rates in Europe. The city's door-to-door collection system facilitates efficient waste sorting and collection, while its network of recycling centers ensures that materials are properly processed.

Ljubljana's success is underpinned by a strong commitment to public education and participation. The city has implemented initiatives that engage residents in sustainability efforts, such as workshops, campaigns, and educational programs. By fostering a sense of co-responsibility, Ljubljana has empowered its citizens to take an active role in waste management, contributing to the city's overall success.

In the Middle East, Dubai is making strides in urban waste management through its integrated waste management strategy. The city has invested in state-of-the-art waste treatment facilities, including a large-scale waste-to-energy plant that converts waste into electricity. Dubai's strategy also includes initiatives to reduce plastic waste, with a focus on promoting reusable alternatives and enhancing recycling infrastructure.

Dubai's approach is characterized by its use of technology and innovation to optimize waste management processes. Smart waste collection systems, equipped with sensors and data analytics, enable efficient route planning and reduce operational costs. Public awareness campaigns and educational programs further support Dubai's efforts, encouraging residents to adopt sustainable waste practices and contribute to the city's environmental goals.

These case studies illustrate the diverse approaches cities around the world are taking to address the challenges of urban waste management. While each city has its unique context and challenges, common themes emerge, such as the importance of public engagement, policy innovation, and technological advancement. By learning from these success stories, other cities can develop tailored strategies that align with their specific needs and resources, paving the way for more sustainable and effective waste management practices.

The journey to successful urban waste management is complex and multifaceted, requiring collaboration, creativity, and commitment. As cities continue to grow and evolve, the importance of sustainable waste solutions will only increase. By embracing innovation and fostering a culture of environmental responsibility, urban centers can transform their waste management systems into models of sustainability, ensuring a cleaner, healthier future for generations to come.